2505

9.2   3 points

Artificial

Satellites

Artificial
Satellites

Ray Spangenburg and Kit Moser

Franklin Watts

A DIVISION OF GROLIER PUBLISHING
NEW YORK · LONDON · HONG KONG · SYDNEY
DANBURY, CONNECTICUT

For
JOHN RHEA,
and the great days at
SPACE WORLD MAGAZINE

Photographs ©: AP/Wide World Photos: 35 (Dexter Cruez), 54 (Reed Saxon); Corbis-Bettmann: 25 left (UPI), 77; NASA: cover, 8, 10, 11, 14, 16, 23, 27, 47, 56, 65, 70, 71, 74, 96, 98, 102, 124, 127; Photo Researchers: 72, 87, 88, 89, 111 (Julian Baum/SPL), 92, 93, 108 (David Ducros/SPL), 59, 120 (Geospace/SPL), 100 (NASA/Russian Space Agency/SS), 66 (Wesley); Photri/NASA: 2, 33, 34, 38, 49, 51, 80, 104, 114; Sovfoto/Eastfoto: 20, 21, 25 right; Tom Stack & Associates: 42, 119 (Aerospace Corp.), 17, 83 (NASA/Airworks), 91.

The photograph on the cover shows shows the *Hubble Space Telescope* orbiting over the Indian Ocean. The image was taken by an astronaut onboard the Space Shuttle *Discovery*. The photograph opposite the title page shows *Galileo* under construction.

> ## Visit Franklin Watts on the Internet at:
> ## http://publishing.grolier.com

Library of Congress Cataloging-in-Publication Data

Spangenburg, Ray.
    Artificial satellites / by Ray Spangenburg and Kit Moser.
        p. cm.—(Out of this world)
    Includes bibliographical references and index.
    Summary: Describes the wide array of different types of satellites that have been placed in orbit since the launching of *Sputnik 1* in 1957 and the various functions they perform, from communications and weather forecasting to astronomy and spy tasks.
    ISBN 0-531-11760-X   0-531-13971-9 (pbk.)
    1. Artificial satellites—Juvenile literature. [1. Artificial satellites.] I. Moser, Diane, 1944- II. Title. III. Out of this world (Franklin Watts, inc.)

TL796.3 .S63 2001
629.46—dc21   00-027090

GROLIER
PUBLISHING   1 2 3 4 5 6 7 8 9 10 R 10 09 08 07 06 05 04 03 02 01

Acknowledgments

Many people have contributed to *Artificial Satellites* and this series in dozens of different ways. First, we would like to thank Sam Storch, lecturer at the American Museum-Hayden Planetarium, who reviewed the manuscript and made many helpful suggestions. Also, special appreciation to our editor at Franklin Watts, Melissa Stewart, whose steady flow of enthusiasm, creativity, energy, and dedication have infused this series from the beginning. Finally, thanks to the engineers and scientists at NASA Jet Propulsion Laboratory and NASA Ames Research Center for many provocative discussions through the years.

Contents

Glowing hues of sunrise as seen from the Space Shuttle *Columbia* on the morning that the *Chandra X-Ray Observatory* was launched.

Chandra: X-Ray Eye in the Sky

As the astronaut crew set to work, the Space Shuttle *Columbia* seemed to float lazily through space. Far below, the early morning sunlight glinted off Earth's bright blue waters. It would be a fine summer day.

In reality, though, *Columbia* was speeding in *orbit* around the planet. The astronauts inside the Space Shuttle were also keeping a quick pace. They had a big job ahead of them. Today they would launch *Chandra X-Ray Observatory*, the highest-resolution X-ray telescope ever built. This telescope, an observatory in space, would see distant portions of the Universe as no one had ever seen them before.

The astronauts opened the huge doors of the shuttle's cargo bay and checked on the big telescope and the rocket that would lift it into its special, high orbit. The crew members moved carefully through their checklist. They had trained for this mission for many months, and every step was planned down to the minute. If anything went wrong, they were prepared to make the necessary repairs in the airlessness and *microgravity* of the Space Shuttle's cargo bay.

All went smoothly, though. First, the crew raised the 56-foot (17-meter) telescope into position for release. Then they waited anxiously for the final OK from the flight controllers in Houston, Texas, and from the Chandra Operations Control Center in Cambridge, Massachusetts. Soon they received word: "It's a go!"

These five astronauts worked together to launch the *Chandra X-Ray Observatory* from *Columbia*'s cargo bay.

Electrical power cables between *Columbia* and *Chandra* were disconnected. The telescope would run on its own internal battery power until its solar wings could be unfurled and begin collecting power from the Sun. Then astronauts Catherine "Cady" Coleman and Michel Tognini ejected *Chandra* from the cargo bay. It was 6:47 A.M. Commander Eileen Collins and Pilot Jeff Ashby maneuvered *Columbia* away from the telescope just as *Chandra*'s booster rocket ignited.

Chandra was on its way to its final high, oval orbit one-third of the way to the Moon. There, it would observe and record the often-explosive realms visible only through X-ray astronomy. *Chandra* joined the *Hubble Space Telescope* and the *Compton Gamma Ray Observatory* as part of NASA's Great Observatories Program designed to uncover the mysteries of the Universe.

Chandra is a telescope, but it is also a *satellite*—just one of the many artificial satellites that act as our eyes and ears in space. Some satellites study our home planet, while others look outward into the unknown realms of space. All the data satellites collect are relayed back to scientists on Earth.

We live in a very special age—the age of satellites—a time when vast networks of these orbiting machines affect nearly every aspect of our lives. This book tells their story.

Chapter 1

Robots in Orbit

Artificial satellites are space-borne robots that have been placed in orbit by rocket launchers or shuttle crews. Today, more than 1,000 of these highly useful machines perform an endless dance around our planet. They come in many shapes and sizes and perform hundreds of tasks that we have come to take for granted.

Satellites are not limited to this group of high-tech machines that orbit Earth. A satellite is any object that revolves around another object in space. Satellites may be natural objects or "artificial" ones, built by humans. Earth is a natural satellite that orbits the Sun, and the Moon is a natural satellite that orbits Earth. This book focuses on artificial satellites—both those that move around Earth and those we have sent to orbit other planets and the Sun.

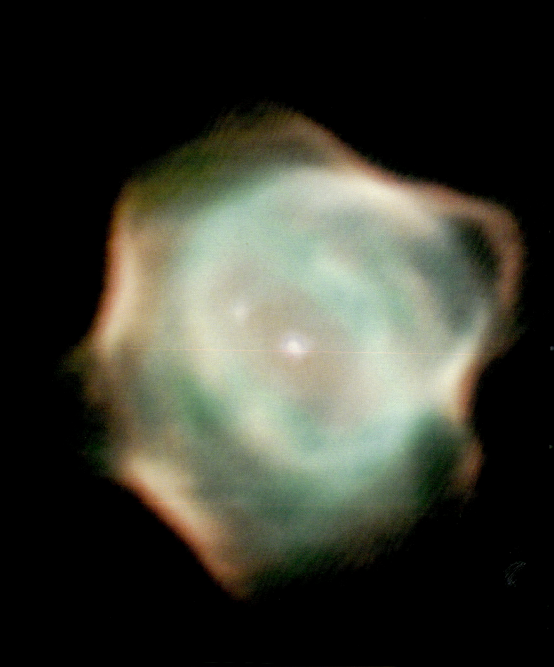

The *Hubble Space Telescope*—one of the most well-known artificial satellites—took this image of the Stingray Nebula.

Hundreds of artificial satellites orbit high above Earth's atmosphere. Each one has a specific job to do. Like mechanical servants, they relay our personal messages and broadcast the news. They observe and listen and report what they see and hear. They keep us informed about our planet by monitoring the atmosphere, the oceans, and the land. They even provide us with detailed maps of our world and help us understand how Earth formed and how it has changed since then.

Other satellites look outward and report what's happening in the rest of the Universe. They see *nebulae*, galaxies, and stars. They show us matter swirling around *black holes*. These "space-based" observatories help scientists explore important questions about the beginnings of the Universe, its size, its nature, and how it has changed over time.

A few crewed satellites have also joined the flock of automated robots. These include the Space Shuttle orbiters and the *International Space Station*. There have also been other space stations in the past. *Skylab*, a laboratory in space, orbited Earth from 1973 to 1979. It provided living and working areas for three astronauts at a time. The astronauts onboard *Skylab* studied the Sun and performed scientific experiments to learn more about microgravity.

Russian cosmonauts and multinational crews spent many long-duration missions aboard a series of space stations called Salyut between 1970 and 1986. A more complex Russian space station named *Mir* began orbiting Earth in 1986. Its flight has lasted more than 14 years. During that time, *Mir* has hosted many scientific experiments and long-duration space missions, including several visits by representatives from the United States and other nations.

Satellites sent to orbit other planets have mapped the surfaces of such distant worlds as Mars and Venus. A satellite named *Galileo* has surveyed

This image of the *Skylab Space Station* was taken by astronauts aboard the *Skylab 4* spacecraft.

Galileo was launched from the payload bay of the Space Shuttle *Atlantis.*

the mysterious, far-off moons of Jupiter. Another, *Cassini*, is due to begin exploring the neighborhood of the ringed planet Saturn in 2004.

In thousands of ways, satellites have made human life easier and more efficient. They have also expanded human knowledge about the world we live in and the Universe we are part of. They have transformed both the way we live and the way we think about the Universe.

Features of a Satellite

Most satellites have a few basic features in common. These include radar for measuring altitude, solar cells for generating power from the Sun's energy, and batteries (rechargeable by the solar cells) for use when the Sun is hidden behind Earth. Many satellites also have devices that allow scientists and engineers on Earth to shift the orientation of sensors or antennas or adjust the satellite's position so that it stays in a particular orbit. Most satellites also have equipment that monitors the "health" of the satellite and its instruments.

Depending on the satellite's purpose, it may have various other instruments onboard. A satellite that is surveying land formations or natural resources on Earth carries imaging devices, such as cameras and *spectrometers*. Communications satellites have radio transmitters and receivers for sending and receiving signals. A navigation satellite must be capable of supplying a stable radio signal source.

Satellites are positioned in various orbits, depending on their purposes. Orbits may be close to Earth (Low Earth Orbit, or LEO) or high. Some are synchronized with Earth's movement, so that they always stay above the same location on Earth.

Orbits may be circular or they may be *eccentric*, tracing a long oval path. In an eccentric orbit, the satellite sometimes travels close to Earth and sometimes farther away. A satellite's orbit may send it around the equator or sling it over a polar region. Often, satellites travel at an angle to Earth's lines of longitude.

Satellite Orbits

Vital Statistics

Altitude Band	Types of Satellites in Band
LOW EARTH ORBIT 90 to 300 miles (145 to 483 km)	Imaging, reconnaissance, and scientific satellites; crewed spacecraft
HIGHLY ECCENTRIC ORBIT	Some communications, surveillance, and science satellites, especially those that need to pass over northern and polar areas
300 TO 630 MILES (483 to 1,014 km)	Earth observation and weather satellites, also some navigation and surveillance satellites
630 TO 1,250 MILES (1,014 to 2,012 km)	A wide cross-section of types, including military surveillance, electronic monitoring, and surveillance satellites
6,200 TO 13,700 MILES (9,978 to 22,048 km)	Navigational satellites
21,750 TO 22,370 MILES (35,000 to 36,000 km)	*Geosynchronous* satellites, including broadcast, communications, data relay, surveillance, and weather observation

The First Satellite

The first artificial satellite, *Sputnik 1*, began orbiting Earth on October 4, 1957. *Sputnik 1* was launched by the former Soviet Union. Also known as the Union of Soviet Socialist Republics (USSR), the Soviet Union included present-day Russia, Ukraine, Belarus, and several other countries in eastern Europe and central Asia.

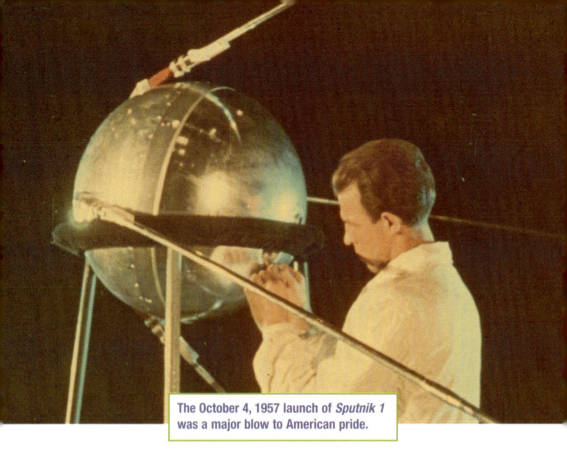

Sputnik 1 was small—only about 24 inches (61 centimeters) across and weighing 184 pounds (83 kilograms). Despite its size, *Sputnik 1* proved an important point: Humans could create an artificial satellite and put it in orbit around Earth.

The launch also gave the Soviet Union an opportunity to demonstrate its rocket power and technological advancement. The world did not fail to take notice.

At the time, the Soviet Union and the United States were not on friendly terms. Since the end of World War II (1939–1945), the two countries had been engaged in a "Cold War." Instead of fighting a "hot" war with bullets, the two rivals stockpiled nuclear weapons and competed ferociously for international prestige.

The governments of both countries reasoned that showing strength and the ability to meet difficult technological challenges would translate into respect for their military power on Earth. The launch of *Sputnik 1* came as a major blow to the United States.

By November 3, the Soviets had done it again. Now a second satellite, *Sputnik 2*, was circling the globe. The second satellite was much heavier, weighing 1,121 pounds (508 kg). *Sputnik 2* carried a small dog named Laika—the first living creature to orbit beyond Earth's atmosphere in the weightlessness and vacuum of space. Unfortunately, the Soviet Union had no way to bring Laika safely back to Earth, so the little dog died in space.*

Sputnik 2 carried a dog named Laika into space.

* Former Soviet space administrators have since expressed regret about sending Laika into space without the means to get her back.

The Space Race Begins

With the launch of the two Sputnik satellites, the Cold War between the United States and the Soviet Union developed into an intense "space race." In the beginning, both the Soviet and U.S. space programs had military objectives as well as public relations aims. The whole world recognized that rockets lobbed into space could launch warheads just as easily as they launched satellites.

During World War II, the Nazi army used primitive V-2 rockets to bomb Great Britain and other Allied countries with conventional ammunition. At the end of the war, the U.S. government invited the German engineers who built the V-2 rocket to live and work in the United States. Led by rocket expert Wernher von Braun, the team was working feverishly to develop more sophisticated rockets that could launch objects into space. Having knowledgeable German engineers in the United States was a huge technological advantage, but it was a disadvantage in terms of public relations. The team had once worked for Nazi Germany, and the bombs they built had killed many innocent people.

Now the United States wanted to catch up with the Soviet Union in space, and President Dwight D. Eisenhower had to decide whether to use the new rocket built by von Braun and his team.

Ironically, the United States probably could have launched a satellite before the Soviets. Thanks to the help of Wernher von Braun and his team, by 1957, the U.S. Army had built a rocket powerful enough to carry a satellite into space. It was called the Jupiter-C. Politics had stood in the way, though.

President Eisenhower was aware that the world was watching, and he wanted the first U.S. satellite launch to be a contribution to science, not a blunt display of military power. He believed that using an Army

Rocket engineer Wernher von Braun designed many of the most powerful U.S. launch vehicles.

Scientists and engineers had long known that the key to space was rocket power. As the Soviets showed with *Sputnik 1* and *2*, launching a satellite takes speed and power. The satellite must escape Earth's atmosphere, where friction causes drag. Then it must achieve orbit at a horizontal velocity of 17,500 miles (28,164 km) per hour.

If you could throw a ball that fast, it would not fall back to Earth as a ball usually does. Instead, your ball would arc across the sky and enter space. However, it would travel just slowly enough so that the pull of Earth's gravity would keep it from soaring off to some other part of the Universe.

Earth's surface would curve away from your ball's horizontal path as fast as Earth's gravity would pull it down. As a result, the ball would enter orbit, where it would stay indefinitely unless something disturbed it. The higher the altitude the ball achieved, the more slowly it would orbit, and the longer it would take to complete a trip around Earth. The same is true for satellites. The greater a satellite's altitude, the longer it takes to orbit Earth. No person is strong enough to throw a ball into orbit, though—that's a job for a *multistage* rocket.

Early in the twentieth century, Russian theorist Konstantin Tsiolkovsky wrote that multistage rockets would be necessary to achieve orbit. The great American rocket pioneer Robert Goddard launched his first rocket in 1908 and his first two-stage rocket in 1914.

Tsiolkovsky and Goddard realized that a rocket had to attain very high speeds to achieve Earth orbit. They also knew that for greater speed and altitude the rocket would require more fuel. The more fuel a rocket carries, though, the more power it needs to get off the ground. In a single-stage rocket, all the fuel is used up lifting the entire mass of the rocket, its remaining fuel, and empty fuel tanks.

A multistage rocket combines the power of two or more rockets to lift the payload, or cargo, it carries. The rockets may be arranged in several different

rocket to launch a scientific satellite would be a public relations error—especially since the rocket was built by the same men who had built the V-2 rockets for the Nazis. So Eisenhower asked the Navy's scientific laboratory—the Naval Research Laboratory—to develop a rocket for the job. Now he asked the Navy to speed up production on its Viking rocket.

Russian theorist Konstantin Tsiolkovsky (left) and American scientist Robert Goddard (right) made major contributions to the development of rocket technology.

ways, but one of the most common arrangements fires them in series, one after the other. The main engine lifts the payload and other rockets from Earth's surface. When all its fuel is consumed, the empty rocket is *jettisoned*, or ejected. Then, the next rocket, or *booster*, takes over—but it has the advantage of starting at the speed where the first rocket left off and it is lifting less weight. The final speed of the last rocket in a multi-stage rocket is equal to the sum of the final speeds of all the rockets. So the speed achievable from the same amount of fuel is much greater than with a single rocket.

The Navy moved quickly, and by December 6, 1957, just a month after the launch of *Sputnik 2,* all seemed ready. Hopes were high as reporters gathered. The Viking rocket stood on the launchpad, with its little "passenger"—the *Vanguard* satellite—in place. The countdown began. The moment of liftoff arrived, and the Viking roared. The tall, slender rocket slowly lifted a few inches, hovered, and then suddenly crumpled to the ground in a disastrous heap of fire, smoke, and metal. The *Vanguard* satellite fell to the ground and rolled away.

It was not a good beginning. In the minds of Americans and their allies, the space race staked freedom, democracy, and capitalism against the power of a communist dictatorship. The failure of the Viking rocket and its tiny *Vanguard* satellite was especially crushing.

Ready and Waiting

Meanwhile, von Braun's team was ready. These men had more experience with rockets than anyone in the world. For many of them, the dream of space had driven their interest in rockets since boyhood. They also recognized that they had a chance to save the United States from embarrassment and take their adopted homeland into a new era, an age of space. They rapidly completed modification of the Army four-stage Jupiter-C rocket, which had been renamed *Juno 1* (in honor of the Roman god Jupiter's wife).

Meanwhile, a team of engineers at the Jet Propulsion Laboratory (JPL) in Pasadena, California, worked on the satellite. *Explorer 1* was 6.7 feet (2 m) long and only a little more than 6 inches (15.2 cm) in diameter. It was bigger than *Vanguard*, but much smaller than either of the two *Sputnik* satellites. This size difference did not escape the world's notice, but at this point the United States was eager to enter space, and a small satellite took less rocket power to launch. So the United States focused on science. James Van Allen, a professor at the University of Iowa, designed a series of scientific experiments that fit neatly inside the little capsule.

Finally, everything was ready. On January 31, 1958, less than 4 months after the launch of *Sputnik 1*, the first U.S. satellite soared into space. During its voyage, *Explorer 1* collected scientific information

A group of technicians prepares the first U.S. satellite *Explorer 1* for launch in 1958.

about cosmic rays, micrometeorites, and temperatures up to an altitude of about 1,580 miles (2,543 km). It also found a belt of radiation that lies trapped between 620 and 3,000 miles (998 and 4,828 km) above Earth's equator. This region is now known as the first of the Van Allen Belts, named after the scientist who designed the experiment that discovered them.

The United States had arrived in space with its first orbiting satellite.

An Agency for Space

The race continued. Only one of the next three U.S. launches succeeded. It sent the first *Vanguard* soaring into space in March 1958. Meanwhile, Soviet scientists and engineers were busy. *Sputnik 3* reached orbit in May. This satellite weighed 2,978 pounds (1,351 kg). It was much bigger and more impressive than any previous satellite.

The United States and the Soviet Union seemed to be playing out a pageant that pitted their competing ideologies against each other before the rest of the world. By July, President Eisenhower had laid the groundwork for a new agency—the National Aeronautics and Space Administration (NASA)—which began operating on October 1, 1958. By December, NASA had announced the Mercury Program, which would put the first American astronauts in space.

Meanwhile, NASA continued to lob satellites into space with regularity—and their uses rapidly went beyond just demonstrating military might. They soon became extraordinarily useful. The first communications satellite, *SCORE*, beamed a recorded message from President Eisenhower on December 18, 1958. It was really just a public relations demonstration, since the satellite served little purpose after the tape was played. However, within 2 years, the first passive communications satellite, *Echo 1*, was launched.

Kinds of Satellites

Kind	Job	First Launched by U.S.	Year
SCIENTIFIC	Collect scientific information about the upper atmosphere	*Explorer 1*	1958
WEATHER	Collect information useful for forecasting weather	*TIROS 1*	1960
COMMUNICATIONS	Transmit a recorded voice from space	*SCORE*	1958
	Relay messages from point to point on Earth's surface	*Echo 1*	1960
NAVIGATION	Locate objects on Earth's surface	*TRANSIT 1B*	1960
MILITARY	U.S. reconnaissance of Soviet missile-launching sites and silos	*SAMOS 2*	1961
EARTH RESOURCES SURVEY	Photograph Earth's surface, providing a record of changes	*Landsat*	1972

An "Echo" of Things to Come

Usually, an echo recalls an event in the past, but the satellite named *Echo* was the start of something new and exciting—the communications revolution. As the first communications satellite, it was the beginning of what is now a multibillion-dollar industry. Today, countries all over the world have their own communications satellites, including India, Japan, Canada, and France. Many of these satellites are owned by consortiums and private enterprise rather than by governments. Together, they link the world as never before.

Other kinds of satellites began soaring into space in the early 1960s. Within a few years, an early version of nearly every kind of satellite we have today was launched into space. Navigation satellites, weather satellites, military spy satellites and satellites that surveyed Earth's resources reported their findings. The age of satellites had begun.

Chapter 2

Linking the World Together

Back when people lived in caves, they knew how to communicate, but they could reach only a small audience—those within view or earshot. A glare meant, "Don't you dare!" A mellow grunt might mean, "That meal was good." Eventually, people learned to send signals to faraway listeners with drumbeats or visual signals, such as puffs of smoke.

Today, we have systems that can carry complicated ideas and thoughts much, much farther than a drumbeat. You can use a graph to show the results of a complicated science experiment. You can convey a feeling with a photograph or a recorded song. All these images and sounds can be sent to the other side of the world in minutes via satellite. That's the magic of modern technology.

How a Communications Satellite Works

Most communications satellites and many weather satellites move in a *geostationary* orbit. In that orbit, a satellite seems to remain in one position, or stationary, above Earth's surface. It is positioned in a circular orbit 22,300 miles (35,880 km) above Earth's equator, and it moves at exactly the right speed to remain "in sync" with Earth. In fact, this special orbit is sometimes called a geosynchronous orbit. A satellite in this orbit appears to be motionless because it stays above one spot on Earth at all times.

A geostationary satellite has a direct line of sight to about one-third of Earth's surface at any given time. That's one reason this orbit is perfect for communications satellites—it's high enough to "hear" on a direct line from two widely distant points. When two points on Earth's surface are too far away, one satellite can relay the information to another satellite for delivery.

A simple communications satellite relays a received signal directly to a ground station or another satellite without changing it. Today's communications satellites are usually more sophisticated, though. They receive the signal, and then amplify or improve it before passing it on.

You can transmit almost anything electronically that you can communicate in person—and that is one of the miracles of life in the twenty-first century. When you talk to a friend, you're communicating. When you talk on the phone, you're using electronic communications. If you're sending or receiving messages or pictures over long distances or over mountains, chances are you're using a satellite.

Daily life on Earth has changed dramatically in just the past few decades, thanks to the visionaries who were quick to see the possibilities. Short-wave radios bounce radio waves off the atmosphere, but the results are spotty and unpredictable. Satellites beam signals to Earth from orbit, and the results are usually amazingly clear and dependable.

In 1960, NASA launched *Echo 1*, a 100-foot (30.5-m) aluminum-coated balloon that began the communications satellite business. It was developed by Bell Telephone Laboratories and was first conceived

Echo 1, the first communications satellite, was developed by Bell Telephone Laboratories and sent into orbit in 1960.

The *Telstar 1* communications satellite was the first privately built satellite.

by a man named John Pierce, who is known as the "father of communication satellites."

Echo 1 was the first satellite to allow two-way communication by reflecting either voice or television signals from its surface. It relayed two-way voice messages between transmitters in Iowa and Texas, and Bell Labs sent the first intercontinental satellite signal across the Atlantic Ocean. The experiment was a success.

This technology soon attracted the attention of the communications industry, and AT&T (the American Telephone and Telegraph Corporation) joined Bell Labs in developing the first commercial satellite. *Telstar 1* was launched in 1962. *Telstar* transmitted a live television

Arthur C. Clarke: Odyssey into the Future

We take communications satellites for granted now, but in 1945 most people had never even thought of the possibility. So when an article by a young science buff predicted an advanced communications satellite system that would relay radio and television signals around the world, most people thought he was just another young dreamer.

Author and scientist Arthur C. Clarke

The young science buff was Arthur C. Clarke, and 20 years after his article appeared in a magazine called *Wireless World*, the *Early Bird* geostationary satellite was launched. Today, the geostationary orbit where most communications satellites "live" is also known as the "Clarke Belt."

Born in England in 1917, as a teenager Clarke mapped the Moon using a telescope that he built himself. He also joined the British Interplanetary Society, a small group of forward-thinking people who investigated and promoted ideas about space travel. After World War II, Clarke studied physics and mathematics at King's College, graduating in 1948. He soon combined a talent for writing with his love of science and adventure and began writing science-fiction stories, essays, and novels. He rapidly became one of the best-known figures in the world of science fiction.

Many of Clarke's stories have become motion pictures. "The Sentinel" became the basis for one of the greatest science-fiction movies of all time—*2001: A Space Odyssey*. Still writing today, Clarke continues to fascinate both scientists and lay people with his exciting and challenging visions of the future. Now in his eighties, he remains a strong and vocal advocate for space exploration.

signal across the Atlantic on its first day of operation. The transmission left the United States, traveled to Great Britain and France, and then back again, relayed by the satellite.

Communications Satellite "Firsts"

Satellite	Description	Launched
PROJECT SCORE	First voice message broadcast relayed from space	1958
ECHO 1	First telecommunications satellite	1960
TELSTAR 1	Television programs relayed between the United States and Europe; first commercially financed telecommunications satellite (AT&T)	1962
SYNCOM 2	First geostationary satellite	1963
SYNCOM 3	First trans-Pacific television transmission shows Olympic Games opening in Tokyo to U.S. viewers	1964
EARLY BIRD (INTELSAT 1)	First international commercial television communications satellite also included telegraph and telephone circuits	1965
ANIK A1 (TELSAT 1)	Canada's first communications satellite	1972
SAKURA/CS	Japan's first communications satellite	1977
STW/CHINA (DONG FANG HONG 15)	China's first telecommunications satellite in geostationary orbit	1984
MORELOS 1	Mexico's first telecommunications satellite, launched from the Space Shuttle	1985

Vital Statistics

Satellite	Description	Launched
AUSSAT	First of a three-satellite telecommunications system for Australia, launched from the Space Shuttle	1985
DBS-1	Direct television broadcasting from a satellite to homes in North America	1993

Echo was a passive satellite—signals simply bounced off its smooth surface and back to Earth. *Telstar* was a more sophisticated active-repeater communications satellite. It carried a *transponder*—a receiver that could also transmit on a programmed signal. It moved around Earth in a low, eccentric orbit, and it could carry either one television signal or six telephone calls at once. The satellite was powered by 3,600 solar cells on the exterior and nickel-cadmium batteries inside.

Telstar's capabilites intrigued the world. Soon many other groups began working on communications satellites. Within a year, NASA and the U.S. Department of Defense had launched the first Syncom (*syn*chrononous *com*munications) satellite into geosynchronous orbit. *Syncom 1* didn't function, but *Syncom 2*, positioned above Brazil, succeeded in July 1963. *Syncom 3* went to work the following year in a position above the equator between the United States and Japan. In an exciting first, U.S. television viewers watched the 1964 Olympic Games open in Tokyo, broadcast across the Pacific Ocean via satellite. *Syncom 3* also relayed some signals to another satellite, *Relay 2*, to television viewers in Europe.

It wasn't long before many other communications and broadcast satellites followed. The world was getting smaller.

Information, Please

Today, many countries have their own communications satellites. These include Canada's Anik series and Russia's Moniya series. INTELSAT, formed in 1964, is a group of more than 125 nations. It

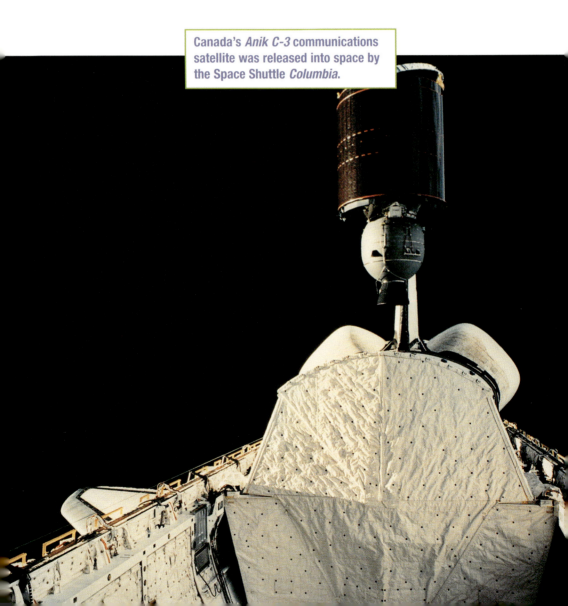

Canada's *Anik C-3* communications satellite was released into space by the Space Shuttle *Columbia*.

has launched and maintains a vast system of communications satellites capable of relaying a variety of signals including telephone, television, facsimile (fax), and telex. Its nonprofit services are used by more than 180 countries and regions around the world. Many private companies have also built and launched satellites. One example is Western Union's Westar satellite.

People all over the world rely on receiving information relayed by satellites. When you talk on the telephone to someone across town or across the country, a satellite may be relaying the message. When you look up information on the World Wide Web, data may be relayed to your modem line via satellite. You may also watch satellite-relayed television programs.

Since the 1960 launch of *Echo 1*, communications satellites have created a world where distance and remoteness no longer block the exchange of information, goods, and services. The global community has arrived.

Chapter 3

Where Are We?

The U.S. Navy was quick to jump onto the satellite bandwagon by launching the first navigation satellites. A navigation satellite is really just a highly specialized kind of communications satellite. Using navigation satellites, the Navy's ships can precisely track their positions as they plow through the open ocean far from any landmarks.

A navigation satellite can provide a reference so that an aircraft or a ship—or even an individual—can establish its position on Earth's surface. Early navigation satellites used the principle of the Doppler shift. Technicians onboard a ship would note the shift in the satellite's frequency to determine the ship's longitude and latitude.

How Science Works: The Doppler Shift

Have you ever noticed that the sound of a truck coming toward you on the freeway changes as the truck gets closer? The pitch keeps getting higher and higher as the truck approaches. After the truck passes you, the pitch drops lower and lower as the truck moves farther and farther away. The same thing happens with other moving sounds, such as a train whistle. This change in the pitch of moving sound waves as an object approaches or recedes from the listener is called the "Doppler shift," or the Doppler effect. It is named after the Austrian scientist Christian Johann Doppler.

We experience the Doppler effect because as a whistling locomotive, for example, moves toward the listener or observer, the sound waves get crowded together in front of the train. As a result, more waves arrive at the listener's ear than would arrive if the train were standing still. As the locomotive moves away, the listener receives fewer sound waves in a given amount of time than would be heard if the train were stationary.

To use early navigation satellites, people measured shifts in radio waves from the orbiting satellites to determine their own position.

Global Positioning System

The U.S. military needed more accurate positioning and navigation information, so government scientists developed a sophisticated system called the NAVSTAR Global Positioning System (GPS). At first, GPS was available only to authorized military and government users. Today, though, anyone with a GPS receiver can use the system to find his or her precise location on Earth. The system can be used by someone on foot, in a car, in a plane, or on a boat. It works equally well in the middle of a city, deep in a forest, and on the high seas. If you have a GPS receiver, the motto goes, you'll never be lost again.

GPS has a variety of applications. It can be used to navigate all kinds of vessels, whether used by the military, commercial companies, or ordinary people out sailing in a boat, piloting a plane, or hiking on a mountainside.

The Global Positioning System's accuracy far surpasses previous navigation satellite systems. This is how it works: A web of twenty-four NAVSTAR satellites in 12-hour orbits form the heart of the system. They orbit Earth at an altitude of 12,500 miles (20,117 km). Their

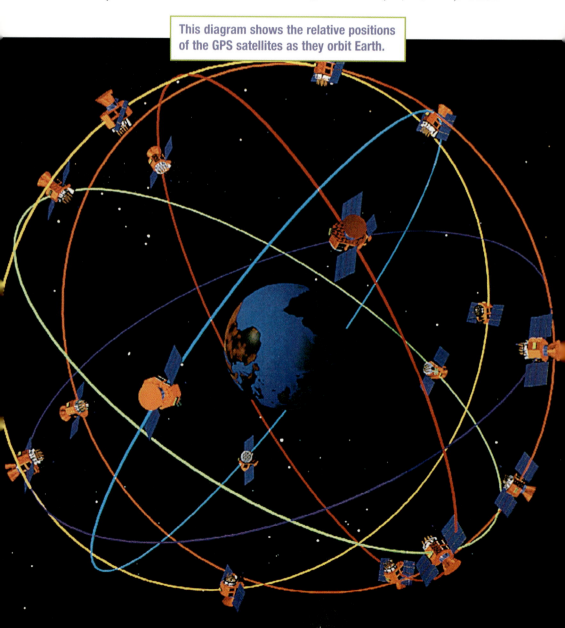

This diagram shows the relative positions of the GPS satellites as they orbit Earth.

positions in orbit are tightly controlled, and they carry highly accurate clocks. The system knows the speed of the satellites' radio signals, and it knows the positions of the satellites. Positions on Earth's surface are calculated by comparing the travel time for signals to a GPS receiver from at least three satellites. Once the receiver's position is identified, the person or vessel holding the receiver is located—within about 50 yards (46 m). When a GPS ground station (signal receivers positioned on the ground) can also be used, accuracy increases dramatically—to within a few inches.

The Lay of the Land

GPS has brought dramatic changes to the ancient science of surveying. For centuries, surveyors have climbed mountainsides and hiked through forests to measure distances and make detailed notations for accurate positioning and mapmaking. Today, the NAVSTAR Global Positioning System allows surveyors to determine position by using the coordinates and time signals from the satellite network. Surveyors still need to position GPS signal receivers on the ground in the locations they want to survey, but the satellite network has greatly simplified the process and improved the accuracy of the measurements.

To use the system for surveying, a receiver on the ground picks up signals from three or more of the satellites in the network. The time-pulsed signals from one of the satellites are used to measure the distance to that satellite, and that information is combined with the distances to the other satellites. Using all this information, computers can determine the latitude, longitude, and elevation of the receiver. The accuracy of the final measurements depends on the quality of the receiver and the number of satellites that can be used for that location. Overall, the surveying measurements achieved through GPS are highly useful.

Iceberg Watch

In the early 1990s, an iceberg the size of Rhode Island snapped off Antarctica. Known as B10A, this big drifting chunk of ice towered about 300 feet (91 m) above the water and may have extended as far as 1,000 feet (305 m) below. Using traditional tracking techniques, scientists followed the iceberg's movements for several years. They looked on as chunks broke off the giant iceberg and drifted northeast, between Antarctica and Tierra del Fuego at the tip of Argentina.

Then the iceberg suddenly broke in half! The usual methods of tracking—visual sightings, surface radar, and regular satellite images—no longer worked. The big iceberg disappeared from view during a period of dark, cloudy winter weather. A ship sent to the iceberg's last known position couldn't find it either. Finally, a radar instrument called SeaWinds spotted the iceberg in July 1999. The SeaWinds radar was located onboard a NASA satellite named *QuikScat*.

NASA and the SeaWinds science team recognized that the remains of B10A could pose a threat to boats in international shipping lanes. Using radar tracking day and night, the SeaWinds instrument kept watch over the ice slabs to prevent collisions with ships.

The science team also used the opportunity to study the breakup of a major iceberg. It was a rare opportunity to observe the effects of ocean winds and climate on melting polar ice. The polar regions play an important part in regulating Earth's climate, and using the Sea-Winds radar to watch B10A gave experts a chance to observe this chunk of polar ice from an unusual view.

So, like many other satellites, *QuikScat* and its instruments play many roles. They help us understand the Earth we live in, survive in our environment, and, in this case, navigate safely.

Major Navigation Satellites

Satellite	Description	Launched
TRANSIT 1B	First satellite dedicated to navigation	1960
TRANSIT 4A	First satellite to use a nuclear mini-generator	1961
TRANSIT 4B	Tested a method for using Earth's gravity to position satellites	1961
COSMOS 192	First Soviet navigation satellite	1967
NAVSTAR	First satellite launched for the NAVSTAR system, a navigation system used to provide positions on a continuous basis	1978
GLONASS 1	The first in a series of Soviet satellites similar to NAVSTAR	1982
GLONASS 786	One of three Russian GLONASS navigation satellites put into operation in January 1999*	1998
GPS IIR-3	Forty-sixth NAVSTAR satellite, launched in October to replace aging satellite in operation since 1990	1999

* According to GLONASS data

Earth
Watch

When we saw the first images of Earthrise from the Moon, our view of our planet changed forever. These pictures helped us recognize Earth's fragility. In the last few decades, we have sent an array of spacecraft to other planets. We have learned a lot about our neighbors, but we have also learned a lot about our home planet. Looking at other worlds has helped us to appreciate the uniqueness of Earth's oceans and atmosphere.

Studying the out-of-control greenhouse effect taking place on Venus has helped us understand the dangers of releasing too much carbon dioxide into Earth's atmosphere. Or, in another scenario, we understand how our planet could become an airless desert like Mars. Earth, we now know, is a tiny and vulnerable part of the vast Uni-

Earthrise, as seen from the surface of the Moon, December 1968

verse—a sort of spaceship on which we travel. We cannot take our planet for granted. It needs our constant care.

In 1989, NASA scientists began to envision an ongoing "Mission to Planet Earth" program that would gather and analyze information about the health and dynamics of our planet's structures and systems. The program, which was originally called the U.S. Global Change Research Program, was designed to keep tabs on all Earth's vital signs.

The original idea involved a fleet of spacecraft to monitor every change in our planet's *biosphere*, that is, the entire Earth, all the organisms that live here, and everything that makes life here possible. Budget cuts have caused the original plan to be restructured, and much of the program's future is uncertain. However, the concept has always been part of NASA's overall goals. In fact, many satellites already provide an impressive amount of scientific data about our home planet.

These satellites predict weather and monitor changes in climate. They also study crops and observe environmental changes caused by vehicles and land use. Most of these satellites are limited to resolutions of about 0.6 miles (1 km), but some can produce images of objects as small as 32.8 feet (10 m) across. *Altimeters* aboard some satellites measure the height of land and sea areas, allowing scientists to track changes in sea levels with great accuracy.

Weather Watchers

"You can talk about the weather, but you can't do anything about it," as the old saying goes, and scientists are still a long way from controlling the weather. However, satellites have caused a revolution in weather forecasting, thanks to pictures and information from geostationary meteorological satellites.

One of NASA's first moves was to put "eyes in the sky" to watch for coming storms. NASA launched its first meteorological (weather) satellite in 1960. *TIROS 1* (Television and Infrared Observation Satellite) was the first of a series of satellites that aimed television cameras at Earth and captured more than 500,000 pictures of worldwide

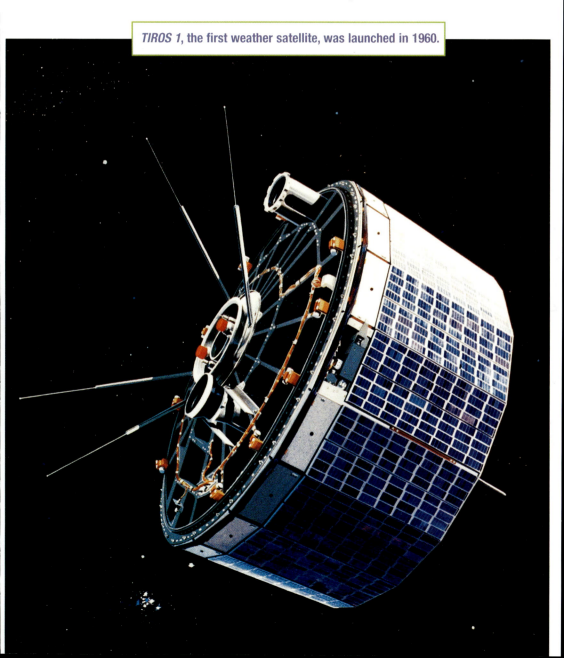

TIROS 1, the first weather satellite, was launched in 1960.

weather systems. Later, NASA developed more sophisticated satellites, known as the Nimbus series.

Before the space age, weather forecasts were mostly educated guesswork. The best sources of information were measurements made by local instruments, the past experience of local observers, and written records.

After 1960, though, meteorologists had an entirely new view of the weather. They were surprised to learn how much of the globe is covered by clouds at any one time. The satellites showed hurricanes forming and moving toward landmasses, and the interaction of warm and cold air. Today, no television weather forecast is complete without full-color weather satellite images that show the locations of cold fronts, high- and low-pressure areas, and storm fronts. If you turn on your computer and connect to the Internet, you can easily get weather data and images for any part of the world.

Today's weather forecasts come from many kinds of information, including satellite images and data, observations from sites around the world, written records of past events, and computer models. Most key information, though, comes from satellites in space.

Most of the information about weather patterns in the United States comes from a series of satellites called *GOES* (Geostationary Operational Environmental Satellite). The first of these satellites was launched in 1975 to collect images of clouds and measure their heights. That information was beamed down to meteorologists on Earth. More recent *GOES* satellites have also provided vertical profiles of temperature and water vapor. *GOES 8*, launched in 1994, can relay images and temperature profiles at the same time.

GOES, a synchronous-orbit weather satellite, provided meteorologists on Earth with information that improved their forecasts.

Other satellites orbit lower, over the poles. A U.S. government scientific agency called NOAA (National Oceanographic and Atmospheric Administration) maintains some of the most important satellites in this category. These satellites can detect small differences in the radiation given off by Earth. From this information, meteorologists can calculate upper air temperatures. They use these calculations to set up computer models that help forecast the weather. In the past, this kind of information could only be collected by instruments carried aloft by weather balloons.

Data from all these satellites help weather forecasters announce more timely storm watches and warnings. When a hurricane, flood, blizzard, or tornado is on the way, every minute counts. Early warnings about severe weather save countless lives. Scientists may not have learned to tame bad weather, but they usually know when it's coming and have some idea about how bad conditions may be when it arrives.

Oceans of Air and Water

Changes in climate come from many sources, but one of the most important is the way Earth's atmosphere interacts with its vast ocean waters. Recently, the governments of the United States and France cooperated on a satellite project known as TOPEX/Poseidon, designed to study this interaction.

By the late 1990s, scientists were using images from the TOPEX/Poseidon satellite to understand a cycle of climate changes called *El Niño* (Spanish for "the child"). El Niño is a warm seasonal ocean current that runs southward along the coast of Peru. Every 4 to 5 years, this current extends farther south, raising water temperatures several degrees above normal.

The results are usually catastrophic. Plankton, fish, and birds die from the warming. Evaporation increases, producing greater rainfall and a period of extensive flooding and extreme weather patterns. During a major El Niño disturbance, the unusual warmth affects other ocean currents, resulting in worldwide consequences. Droughts may occur in some areas and flooding in others throughout North and South America, Europe, and Asia.

Historical records show that this climate change has been going on for hundreds of years. TOPEX/Poseidon tracks the changes in wave height and average sea level that accompany these events. Its reports are helping scientists to predict *El Niño* at least a year in advance. This

Sue Digby: Satellite Link

"**B**eing a woman does not exclude you from interesting jobs," says Sue Digby. "If you have something in mind, just 'go for it.' There may be a few extra hurdles, but with persistence and a small amount of luck, you will make it."

Digby presently works with the TOPEX/Poseidon and Jason 1 satellite projects. In the past, she has held many interesting jobs and lived in places as diverse as England, Greenland, Newfoundland, and Canada. She spent her earliest years in Greenland, where her parents were marine biologists.

Digby first became involved with artificial satellites when she became a sea-ice research assistant for a Canadian satellite program called Radarsat. Her job was to study sea-ice and icebergs using radar data collected from airplanes and ships.

Digby helped plan experiments, performed all kinds of fieldwork, and analyzed results. She later became sea-ice coordinator at the Canada Center for Remote Sensing.

After 9 years at Radarsat, Digby moved to the United States to join her husband. For 2 years, she worked with scientists and engineers on the Cassini Mission to Saturn. Then she returned to her first love—earth science.

She took a job as the head of user services at NASA's oceanographic archive. Now she spends her time figuring out better ways to get satellite information to users and is developing a web page that will describe the TOPEX/Poseidon and Jason 1 projects. "It has some great El Niño/La Niña information," she says with a grin.

early warning helps people in affected areas to adjust crop plans and prepare for El Niño's disasters.

TOPEX/Poseidon has also helped scientists track another current in the same region that sometimes follows *El Niño*. This current is known as *La Niña* (Spanish for "the girl child"), and it causes unusually cold temperatures in the Pacific Ocean near the equator. Scientists

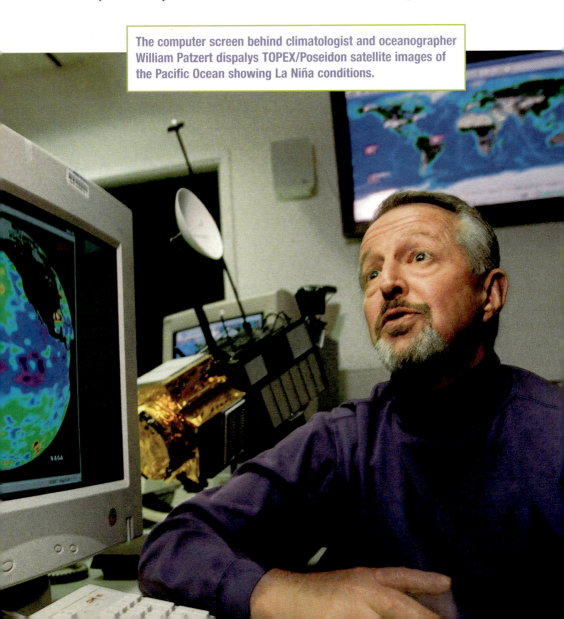

The computer screen behind climatologist and oceanographer William Patzert dispalys TOPEX/Poseidon satellite images of the Pacific Ocean showing La Niña conditions.

believe La Niña may encourage hurricane formation in the Atlantic Ocean. However, La Niña appears less often and is far less destructive than *El Niño*.

The Disappearing Ozone

By the second half of the twentieth century, many environmentalists began raising concerns about the negative changes that human activities have caused in Earth's atmosphere. Satellites provide critical information about ongoing changes in the atmosphere's makeup. From this information, scientists are learning that the atmosphere's chemistry is fragile and can be easily disturbed. Even small changes in chemistry can affect Earth and its inhabitants.

Earth's atmosphere provides the air we breathe, but that's not all. It also protects all living things from the Sun's damaging ultraviolet (UV) rays. Thanks to the atmosphere—especially the ozone layer—living things on Earth have enjoyed a protected existence for a billion years. However, scientists have discovered "a hole" where the protective layer of ozone high in the upper regions of our atmosphere has become thinner.

At first, no one noticed the signs. But by the mid-1980s, scientists looking at satellite images began to see evidence that a hole in the ozone layer had developed above the South Pole. When the scientists looked at older images, they found that *Nimbus 7* had begun recording the change as early as 1973. The hole nearly disappeared during some months, but it returned each year between September and October, and each year the hole grew bigger. The implications were frightening.

Once scientists discovered the hole, they set out to find the causes. They knew a chemical reaction involving energy from the Sun's rays and oxygen in the atmosphere produced the ozone (O_3) layer we depend on. When scientists examined the chemistry of the atmosphere's upper layers, they found that other chemicals were blocking the reaction. One of the culprits proved to be the *chlorofluorocarbons* (CFCs) used in some spray cans and refrigerants.

Additional ozone reports continue to come in from NASA's Total Ozone Mapping Spectrometer (TOMS), which flies aboard *Nimbus 7*. By 1999, the amount of damaging UV rays reaching Earth's surface had risen dramatically, according to NASA's atmospheric scientists.

This computer diagram shows how the level of ozone in the atmosphere above Northern Hemisphere has changed since the late 1970s. The data for this diagram was collected by NASA's Total Ozone Mapping Spectrometer.

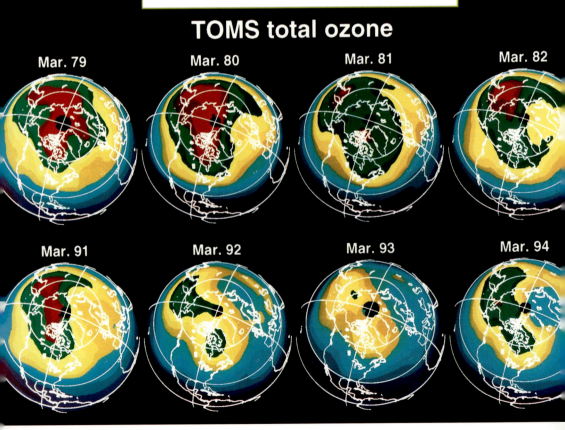

TOMS total ozone

Mar. 79   Mar. 80   Mar. 81   Mar. 82

Mar. 91   Mar. 92   Mar. 93   Mar. 94

Data from TOMS showed that the Northern Hemisphere suffered an average UV increase of almost 7 percent since 1972, and the Southern Hemisphere showed an average rise of just under 10 percent.

By the end of the twentieth century, many of the world's governments had started to restrict the use of CFCs, in the hope of stopping the damage. It's a problem we wouldn't even know about yet without the help of a little satellite named *Nimbus*.

More Clouds and Climate

In December 1999, NASA launched a satellite named *Terra*. It is the flagship—the first satellite—in a planned network of satellites known as the Earth Observing System (EOS). This international program plans to monitor changes in Earth's climate and environment over a 15-year period. Scientists hope to learn how Earth's oceans, lands, air, ice, and life all function together as a total environmental system.

Looking ahead, NASA's Jet Propulsion Laboratory has announced plans to launch a new observatory called *CloudSat* in 2003. This satellite will use advanced radar to study the vertical structure of clouds. (Current weather satellites can catch images of only the topmost layer of clouds.) *CloudSat* will also be the first satellite to look at clouds worldwide, and it will study the transfer of solar energy to and from Earth's atmosphere. The information gathered by *CloudSat* should help us understand climate changes on global, regional, and even local scales.

Looking at the Land

As early as 1972, NASA began to use satellites to watch changes occurring on Earth's surface, in its oceans, and in its atmosphere. The first Earth Resources Technology Satellite (ERTS) was launched that year.

It was the first in a series of satellites that later became more widely known as Landsat satellites. The series has had a long life, and its imaging capabilities continue to give us stunning and beautiful views of Earth from a new vantage point.

Landsat satellites look at the terrain through the eyes of several special instruments. All Landsats have a Multi-Spectral Scanner (MSS) that sees Earth in green, red, and infrared. Each of these views shows the user a different aspect of the terrain. Early Landsats also used a special televisionlike camera that was later replaced by a very high-resolution sensor called a Thematic Mapper (TM).

Digging Up the Past—Remotely

By the 1990s, archaeologists—scientists who study the remains of past civilizations—had begun looking at Landsat images for signs of lost cities, hidden temples, and shrouded reservoirs.

In 1992, satellite images helped archaeologists find the site of the famous Lost City of Ubar in Oman, on the Arabian Peninsula. This outpost was once an assembly point for caravans carrying frankincense across the desert. The site dates to about 2800 B.C. and was occupied until about 300. Tracks leading to the fortress of the lost city showed up on the images, although the structure itself did not.

In 1994, astronauts aboard a different kind of satellite—the Space Shuttle *Endeavour*—trained the Space Radar Laboratory's equipment on the area of Cambodia where the ancient city of Angkor once stood. Evidence suggests that in 1100, this city housed more than a million people. Once the spiritual center of the Khmer people, Angkor contained more than sixty temples, and may have been the largest city in the world at that time. The shuttle images were able to cut through the dense canopy of the tropical rain forest that covers the site and reveal the ruins of Angkor's ancient temples. The images also showed a complex system of canals and reservoirs where water once flowed.

French marine archaeologist Franck Goddio has been using the GPS satellites to map Cleopatra's palace, now submerged beneath the murky waters of the port of Alexandria, Egypt. Archaeologists have also used satellite images to map the public works system used 4,000 years ago by the 20,000 laborers who constructed the pyramids on the Giza Plateau in Egypt.

This Landsat satellite image shows deforestation in Brazil. The dark green of the forested areas contrast with the pale greens and browns of the leveled forest.

Once the images are made, Landsat takes one of three actions. It can send the images directly to Earth, it can store the images and send them to Earth later, or it can relay its images to a network of relay satellites called the Tracking and Data Relay Satellites (TDRS).

Landsat images have a wide range of uses. Scientists use them to monitor environmental changes, pollution, and land-use management. The images have helped people plan large civil-engineering projects, such as dams. They have also provided information about ice floes and the location of natural resources and revealed archaeological remains that no one knew about.

In April 1986, a Landsat satellite passed overhead shortly after a nuclear reactor exploded in Chernobyl in Ukraine, then a part of the former Soviet Union. Within 72 hours, a digital image from Landsat was available worldwide. It showed clearly the cloud of radioactivity that poured into the atmosphere from the reactor following the accident.

Viewing Earth's Biology from Space

In 1998, NASA released images from a continuous year of observing Earth's changing biology on land and sea. Taken by a satellite-based sensor called SeaWiFS (Sea-viewing Wide Field-of-view Sensor), these images trace the "pulse of the planet"—the changing seasons of life— as no set of images ever has before. The mission began when SeaWiFS first began releasing data in September 1997. Scientists originally planned to use it to study only the ocean, but it proved to work equally well in observing changes on land and in the atmosphere.

SeaWiFS observed the impact of El Niño on ocean life and watched the transition that occurred as a result of El Niño's excessive warmth. It also observed the effect of La Niña. Scientists watched blooms of microscopic plants called *phytoplankton* die out under the harsh influence of El Niño. Then they witnessed their incredible rebirth and blooming in the cooled waters brought by La Niña. These blooms stretched from the South American coast across the vast Pacific Basin.

Scientists are currently exploring the role phytoplankton play in the global climate. Like most plants, phytoplankton use carbon dioxide, which they remove from the atmosphere, for photosynthesis. When phytoplankton populations swell, as they did during the 1998 La Niña, scientists suspect the increase in exchange of carbon dioxide may influence some aspects of Earth's climate.

Scientists also observed that phytoplankton blooms affect other sea life. As the bloom from La Niña migrated north, it blocked fish from returning to their usual spawning grounds along the western coast of Alaska. Seabirds in these areas died of starvation because the fish they usually feed on had gone elsewhere.

SeaWiFS also monitors natural disasters, including fires in Florida, Mexico, Canada, Indonesia, and Russia. It has recorded floods in China and dust storms in the Sahara and Gobi Deserts. It has watched hurricanes develop and traced their progress. In the process, SeaWiFS allowed scientists to observe the changing global environment from a unique viewpoint high above the planet.

As Mountains Form

In addition to the useful Earth observations that come from resource imaging satellites, such as Landsat, geologists get information from the Global Positioning System (GPS)—the same network of navigation satellites that makes sure you don't get lost. At present, a group of geologists is watching mountains in the making in southern California.

These geologists have set up sixty GPS receivers in southern California to record the tiny but constant movements that occur along the many earthquake faults in the region. The results are small but significant, leading geologists to conclude that downtown Los Angeles and west Los Angeles are slowly moving east toward the San Gabriel Mountains. The land in between is slowly being compressed. Scientists predict that sometime in the next 1,000 years, new mountains may form to the south. The pace of the movement, the researchers say, is about 0.2 inches (0.5 cm) per year. So don't get out your mountain-climbing gear yet!

Chapter 5

Military Scouts

Although artificial satellites have always had scientific goals, they have also served as military tools. Many historians believe that the Soviet Union launched *Sputnik 1* primarily to show military might and to improve the nation's image. The United States met the Soviet challenge—probably for the same reasons.

The U.S. military continues to use satellites for headquarters-to-field communications, reconnaissance through remote sensing, accurate location of troop positions, and guided weaponry.

Satellites play a key role in the information-gathering and strategic activities of the U.S. military. *Reconnaissance satellites* use a variety of remote-sensing methods to watch or listen from a distance. They may observe movements of troops, tanks, and other artillery, or they may identify the location of arms factories and military stockpiles. They can also conduct extremely detailed photographic surveys of specific geographic areas.*

Other military "spy" satellites focus on communications. Some can even intercept critical conversations among top enemy officials. This is exactly what the United States was able to do during the Serbian war in 1999. Still other artificial satellites can detect nuclear explosions that occur in other parts of the world and warn us when other nations launch strategic missiles.

Most military satellites travel in a polar orbit just a few hundred miles above Earth's surface. This Low Earth Orbit (LEO), combined with state-of-the-art, high-resolution optical devices, enables the satellites to "see" in more detail than satellites traveling in higher orbits. According to some reports, U.S. reconnaissance satellites orbiting 500 miles (805 km) above Earth can distinguish objects as small as 6 inches (15 cm) across.

The presence of these military scouts overhead has made the world a much more public place. Hiding a buildup of military forces or a stockpile of weapons has become much more difficult. It is also difficult to launch a surprise attack. At the same time, defense plans can rarely remain secret.

---

* In the past, these satellites could collect much more detailed information than civilian satellites, such as the Landsat series. Recently, however, private companies have launched satellites that promise to deliver images nearly as detailed as those from military "spy" satellites.

Keeping Track of Junk

The growth of "space junk" should come as no surprise, given the thousands of launches by various countries since 1957. Useless and cast-off equipment, rocket hulls, and defunct satellites whiz overhead at 17,500 miles (28,163 km) per hour, caught forever in orbit around Earth. Occasionally, increased drag causes a satellite to lose momentum and fall out of orbit. Then the satellite plummets unexpectedly back to Earth.

Nearly 9,000 human-made objects orbit Earth. About 30 percent of these objects are satellites, but only about 7 percent are currently working. Another 15 percent are spent rocket bodies, and the remaining objects are fragments and other debris.

The U.S. Space Command of the U.S. Air Force tracks all these objects. It also detects new objects in space and identifies the country that launched it.

When an object in space breaks up, the Space Command predicts the process of decay and determines when the object will fall to Earth and where it will land. Because one of these objects could easily be misinterpreted as an approaching missile warhead and trigger the launch of retaliating missiles, the Space Command warns the international community of an object's impending fall from orbit.

The Space Command also alerts NASA when an object might cross the path of the Space Shuttle or *International Space Station*. Collisions in space are a very real concern. Even though everything in space is weightless, objects retain their *momentum*. This force can do serious damage.

This computer-generated image shows all the catalogued objects orbiting Earth, as seen from a distance of 62,137 miles (100,000 km).

U.S. soldiers use a GPS devices to locate their exact position on the ground.

Military Navigation and Position Information

The U.S. Department of Defense developed the Global Positioning System (GPS) for a variety of military uses. The system can track the movement of enemy troops and note the positions of enemy ships, planes, tanks, and armored vehicles. In addition, U.S. troops and ships use the system in unfamiliar territory.

The Pentagon currently uses GPS to guide precision bombs to their targets when the weather is poor. Future plans call for installation of GPS guidance systems in some 90,000 U.S. gravity bombs by 2008. This kind of precision in weaponry provides a new level of accuracy.

The Future: Space Wars?

As the sophistication of satellite technology has grown, the U.S. military has come to realize that defense of the nation's satellites is rapidly becoming an important issue. The military's own dependence on satellite technology makes satellites even more vulnerable.

For example, an enemy could use lasers to blind the optical sensors on spy satellites or use ballistic missiles to destroy key satellites. Objects as small as buckshot could be lobbed into Low Earth Orbit, where, traveling at orbital speed, they could play havoc with reconnaissance satellites. Commando attacks on ground-control centers and relay stations could also be damaging.

In the early years of the twenty-first century, the U.S. military faces the new challenge posed by a multibillion-dollar investment in space that needs protection, much as ships did on the high seas when navies were formed in the 1700s. The challenge includes devising strategies to protect military capabilities as well as government and private property. Meanwhile, more and more nations have launched their own satellites into space, and the long-standing advantage of the U.S. military in this area has become decidedly narrower.

However, as one representative of the U.S. Space Command has pointed out, aggressively deploying weapons in space could backfire by starting wars. Future military measures and countermeasures must be planned with care.

Chapter 6

Eyes on the Universe

Not all satellites are turned Earthward. Some are turned outward to look at the planets and stars. In 1996, twenty-three space-based telescopes were orbiting Earth, and even more have been added in recent years. One of these is *Chandra*, the X-ray telescope whose launch story appears at the beginning of this book.

These telescopes orbit high above Earth's atmosphere, where they can get a better view of distant objects than telescopes on the ground. On Earth, artificial lights from urban areas drown out the light from the stars. Turbulence and convection in the atmosphere blur images for ground-based telescopes. Water droplets and carbon dioxide interfere with infrared observations, and ozone absorbs UV waves. Orbiting

observatories do not face any of these problems. They can collect unencumbered infrared, X-ray, gamma-ray, or visible-light images of objects in our solar system and beyond.

Seeing in the Infrared

One of the earliest space-based telescopes was the *Infrared Astronomical Satellite* (*IRAS*), which operated for almost a year in 1983. During its survey of the sky, *IRAS* studied the sites of star formation and the

center of our *galaxy*, the Milky Way. The telescope sent back images and data that provided an important base for astronomers to work from, and for the first time, it showed the existence of dust and gas rings around many stars.

Two years later, the European Space Agency launched a follow-up satellite called the *Infrared Space Observatory* (*ISO*). It orbited Earth for 2 years and imaged additional objects that radiate infrared light.

In the early 1990s, the *Cosmic Background Explorer* (*COBE*) stunned the world by looking out almost to the beginning of time with an instrument known as a far infrared absolute spectrophotometer. *COBE*'s most dramatic achievement was its discovery of evidence that provided powerful support for the Big Bang model for the formation of the Universe.

According to the Big Bang model, the Universe originated 10 to 20 billion years ago in an unimaginably violent explosion that created space and time. Such an explosion would have created a uniform cosmic background radiation. The existence of cosmic background radia-

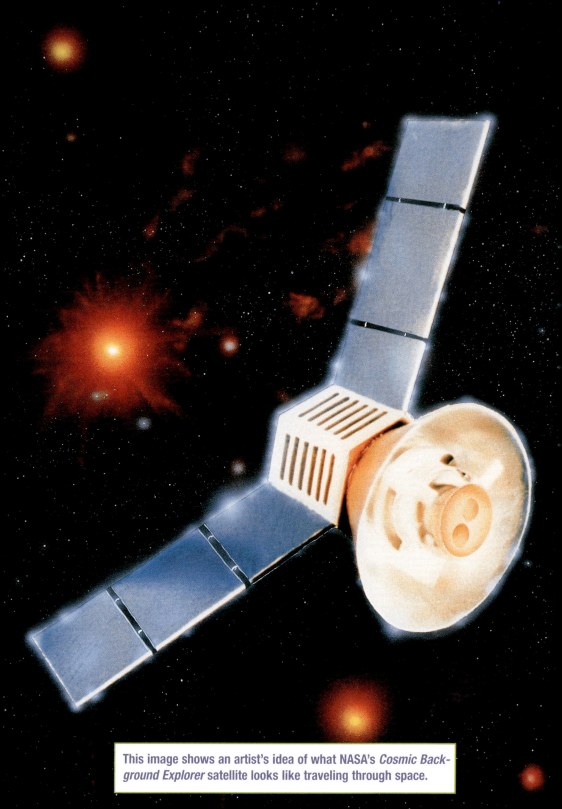

This image shows an artist's idea of what NASA's *Cosmic Background Explorer* satellite looks like traveling through space.

tion was confirmed in 1965 by Arno Penzias and Robert Wilson. *COBE* measured this background radiation at a temperature just slightly above absolute zero.

However, an absolutely uniform background radiation could not have produced the structure we see in the Universe today. This has led scientists to wonder how and when the uniform background radiation that existed at the beginning of space and time developed the irregularities necessary for matter to clump and form such objects as stars and galaxies. An expansion of the Big Bang model, called inflationary theory, addressed this problem. Inflationary theory predicted the existence of minute variations, or "ripples" in the background radiation shortly after the Big Bang.

In 1992, *COBE* discovered areas within the cosmic background radiation that are very slightly warmer or cooler. These differences are extremely small. Scientists attribute these tiny "ripples" in temperature to very slight differences in the density of matter that may have existed early in the development of the Universe. If this line of thought is accurate, the minute variations in density could be a very early stage in the formation of galaxies.

Hubble Space Telescope

In 1990, astronomers welcomed NASA's launch of the *Hubble Space Telescope* (*HST*), named after U.S. astronomer Edwin P. Hubble. Long awaited, this space-based astronomical observatory entered an orbit above the distortion of Earth's atmosphere and had potential for capturing spectacular images of distant objects. Scientists were disappointed when the Hubble's images were not as clear as expected. They quickly realized that the focus of the telescope's main mirror was flawed.

Three years later, astronauts aboard the shuttle orbiter *Discovery* repaired the telescope. As a result, the Hubble's images began to transform ideas and answer questions about the Universe. *HST* could look back 11 billion years, all the way to the dawn of the Universe itself. It

Following a successful maintenance and update visit to the Space Shuttle *Discovery*'s payload bay in December 1999, astronauts took this image of the *Hubble Space Telescope.*

The light we see is only one part of a range of waves known as the *electromagnetic spectrum*. On the short end of the spectrum are gamma rays, X rays, and ultraviolet (UV) rays. In the middle is visible light. On the other end of the spectrum are the long waves of infrared radiation, microwaves, and radio waves.

All these waves are invisible to humans. Yet, we can feel the heat of infrared radiation, and we know we have to protect ourselves from the UV radiation of the Sun. Many satellites carry instruments that can "see" the gamma-ray, X-ray, UV, or infrared radiation that comes from objects. In astronomy, these special instruments reveal aspects of the Universe that are otherwise invisible or very faint.

Gamma rays are produced by nuclear processes, including fission, fusion, and radioactive decay. When astronomers observe gamma rays coming from the sky, they are able to locate objects that are extremely hot and are perhaps in the process of forming heavier chemical elements.

X-ray observations concentrate on objects in space that give off X-ray radiation—also near the short end of the spectrum. X-ray astronomy has unveiled new clues about the large-scale structure of the Universe and has also explored such highly puzzling objects as *pulsars* and black holes.

UV detectors, on the other hand, look at UV radiation, just beyond visible light at the short end of the spectrum, but having a longer wavelength than either X rays or gamma rays.

Infrared radiation has longer wavelengths than visible light, but shorter than microwave radiation or radio waves. All objects with a temperature higher than absolute zero emit some infrared radiation, and some very cool stars actually give off more infrared than visible radiation. So, infrared astronomy is especially good for observing faint or cool objects in space.

The Electromagnetic Spectrum

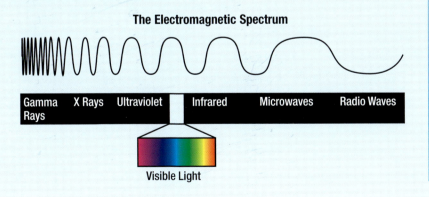

Gamma Rays | X Rays | Ultraviolet | Infrared | Microwaves | Radio Waves

Visible Light

revealed new layers of galaxies—some 40 billion of them—so distant that they had been practically invisible to us before. *HST* also provided the first clear evidence of brown dwarf stars and revealed new information about the birth and death of stars.

HST also captured images of objects a bit closer to home. It found small traces of oxygen present in the atmosphere of Europa, one of Jupiter's moons. It showed us stunning views of the broken pieces of Comet Shoemaker-Levy 9 as they exploded against the cloud-tops of Jupiter in 1993. The telescope also took the best existing photos of Pluto.

Each day, NASA posts stunning *HST* images on the Internet. With a few clicks of a mouse, you can view far-off galaxies, nebulae, double stars, and red giants. Millions of people all over the world have also seen *HST* images in newspapers, magazines, and on television. These pictures show us the complexity and beauty of the Universe.

X-Ray and Gamma-Ray Astronomy

The *Uhuru* (Swahili for "freedom") satellite, launched in 1970 off the coast of Kenya, was the first of three satellites launched by NASA to study objects that emit X rays and gamma rays. Based on data collected by *Uhuru*, astronomers found evidence that galaxies are surrounded by hot, thin gas.

In July 1999, the *Chandra X-ray Observatory* entered orbit from the cargo bay of the Space Shuttle *Columbia*. It quickly began to transform astronomy. Within months after its launch, its images were helping astronomers learn more about how silicon, iron, and other elements are produced during the explosion of a star. *Chandra* has also

Nancy Roman: Star Astronomer

Nancy Roman fell in love with astronomy early in her life. As a fifth-grader in Reno, Nevada, she formed an astronomy club. By the time she entered high school, she knew she wanted to be a professional astronomer. Despite discouragement from many people who couldn't understand why a woman would want to study math and science, she followed her dreams and completed her Ph.D. degree in astronomy at the University of Chicago in 1949.

Throughout the 1960s and much of the 1970s, Nancy Roman was the chief of Astronomy Programs for NASA. In that position, it was her responsibility to plan and oversee many of NASA's astronomy projects. During Roman's career with NASA, she managed the programs for most of the astronomical satellites, including *Copernicus* and *Uhuru*. She also served as program manager for numerous other observing satellites that studied the Universe, including our own Sun and other stars, and she helped develop early plans for the *Hubble Space Telescope*.

After leaving NASA, Nancy Roman continued to encourage young people to go into the sciences. She became a volunteer at the Educational Outreach Program at NASA's Goddard Space Flight Center in Houston, Texas, and taught summer courses for both students and teachers in various colleges and universities.

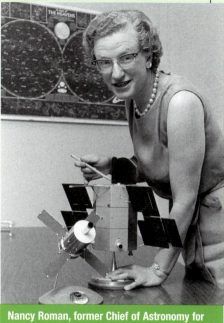

Nancy Roman, former Chief of Astronomy for NASA

captured a glimpse of the violent early phases of a *supernova* and a stunning view of the supernova remnant called Cassiopeia A. *Chandra's* images have begun to provide astronomers with new visions of cosmic explosions and the structures left behind. With these, come fresh clues about the dynamics of these enormous events.

The European Space Agency launched its own X-ray satellite on December 10, 1999. The *XMM* (for X-ray Multi-Mirror) *Observatory* is especially good at detecting very faint X-ray sources. (*Chandra* can see finer detail but has a smaller collecting area.) The *XMM* is expected to be one of the most important space missions of the first decade of the twenty-first century.

Chapter 7

Traveling Beyond Earth Orbit

Not all artificial satellites orbit our home planet. Beginning in the 1960s, NASA has sent dozens of satellites to orbit other worlds. They have traveled to the Moon, Venus, Mars, Jupiter and its four largest moons, Saturn, and the Sun. The former Soviet Union also launched many satellites that have orbited other worlds.

By 2004, a Japanese orbiter will reach Mars. These spacecraft have snapped thousands of photos and collected reams of data. Some have kept hard at work for more than a decade. The information these satellites have gathered and sent back to Earth has taught scientists a great deal about our closest neighbors in the Universe.

The *SOHO* spacecraft provides an ideal vantage point for studying the Sun, its plasma, flares, *corona*, and eruptions.

Checking on the Sun

The Sun's fiery furnace continues to raise enormous questions, and many spacecraft missions have been sent to study its mysteries. Among them are *Ulysses* and *Solar and Heliospheric Observatory* (*SOHO*), two satellites launched in the 1990s.

Ulysses, a joint mission between NASA and the European Space Agency (ESA), was launched in 1990. To study the Sun's polar regions, Ulysses mission planners set the satellite's orbit at especially high solar latitudes. No rocket could possibly achieve this orbit, so *Ulysses* was launched from the Space Shuttle *Discovery*'s cargo bay. From there it set off toward Jupiter. *Ulysses* then took advantage of Jupiter's huge gravitational field to kick its path downward, out of the *ecliptic plane,* where the planets orbit, and over the south polar regions of the Sun.

The orbital path of *Ulysses* varies tremendously. Sometimes it is about 121 million miles (194.5 million km) from the Sun. At other times, it is about 502 million miles (808 million km) away. From this orbit, *Ulysses* can observe areas of the Sun never seen before.

Power Please

The instruments onboard most Earth-orbiting satellites are powered by energy collected from the Sun by solar cells. Since *Ulysses* was headed deep into space (to get a gravity assist from Jupiter), it would have needed giant solar cells to get enough energy for its instruments to operate properly. In fact, it would have needed solar cells so large that no available launch vehicle would have been powerful enough to propel it out of Earth orbit.

To solve this problem, engineers fitted *Ulysses* with a power source called a radioisotope thermo-electric generator (RTG). It's similar to RTGs used to power earlier deep-space missions, such as *Galileo*, launched in 1989. RTGs convert heat, produced by the natural decay of plutonium-238, into electricity.

Ulysses carries nine important instruments, and each one has a specific job. Together, they help scientists learn about solar wind, magnetic fields and particles, interplanetary dust and gas, and cosmic rays. Scientists also use radio data gathered by *Ulysses* to study the Sun's outer atmosphere—the corona—to search the regions between planets for gravitational waves, and to locate the brightest cosmic gamma-ray bursts.

Five years after the launch of *Ulysses,* NASA and ESA collaborated on another big project to study the Sun. The *Solar and Heliospheric Observatory* (*SOHO*) was launched on December 2, 1995. This satellite orbits between the Earth and the Sun at a distance of 932,000 miles (1.5 million km) from Earth. It is positioned at the point where the gravitational pulls of Earth and the Sun are equal.

SOHO gives scientists a long-term, uninterrupted view of the Sun. It also promises to resolve such questions as: What is the Sun like inside? Why is the corona so hot? And what makes the solar wind accelerate?

One of *SOHO*'s jobs is mapping solar flares—sudden rapid and intense variations in brightness. The Sun's magnetic fields vary in strength constantly. Sometimes the field becomes so strong that hot gases fling themselves outward at incredibly high speeds forming the remarkable flares we see.

During its first 4 years in operation, *SOHO* has revealed that, even during this relatively quiet period of the Sun's 11-year cycle of activity, the Sun is much more active than scientists expected. They are eager to find out more as the Sun's activity revs up.

Mapping the Moon

During the 1960s, the United States and the Soviet Union sent several robot missions to the Moon. Some of those spacecraft were orbiters—satellites, that is. They mapped the Moon's surface, studied its topog-

An Apollo command module orbiting the Moon

raphy, and examined its composition. During most of the Apollo missions of the late 1960s and early 1970s, one crew member stayed in the command module and orbited the Moon, while the other two astronauts climbed aboard a lunar module and descended to the Moon's surface. After the last Apollo mission in 1972, no one sent a spacecraft the Moon for more than 20 years.

In the 1990s, two spacecraft traveled to the Moon to become satellites. The first, *Clementine*, was a cooperative effort between NASA and the Strategic Defense Initiative Organization. The spacecraft was launched by NASA on January 25, 1994. The second, *Lunar Prospector*, was launched 4 years later, on January 7, 1998.

The Clementine mission put the spacecraft in orbit around the Moon for a little more than 3 months. During that time, *Clementine* produced the most detailed map we have of the Moon. *Clementine* also tested some new ideas for spacecraft design and development. In the past, NASA had built spacecraft to last a long time. Especially when developing spacecraft that would carry astronauts, safety and survival had always ranked as top priorities. For *Clementine*, though, engineers developed an unusually lightweight design for the structure and propellant systems. The spacecraft was much more fragile than any flown before in space's harsh environment. In additon, the Clementine mission was put together very quickly—it took only 2 years for development from initial concept to launch.

Despite this new design strategy, *Clementine*'s imaging instruments were full-blown. The spacecraft carried five different imaging systems, including a UV/visible camera that captured both UV images and visible-light shots, two types of infrared cameras, and a Hi-Res imager capable of high-resolution imagery. The spacecraft's Star Tracker camera, used primarily for navigation, was also used for imaging.

With these instruments, *Clementine* mapped most of the lunar surface at several resolutions and used wavelengths ranging from UV to infrared. The results stunned planetologists. *Clementine* found high concentrations of hydrogen at the Moon's south pole. Could water ice be hidden in shaded crater floors in this region? The Moon had long been considered a dry and desolate place. Now, the possibility that ice might exist there raised the prospect that the Moon might have resources that could help support a settlement there. Everyone was eager to find out more.

Lunar Prospector arrived at the Moon in 1998. Its mission was to take a close look at the Moon from a low polar orbit and to map the Moon's surface composition. The spacecraft also searched for more evidence of the polar ice deposits that *Clementine's* results had hinted at. *Lunar Prospector* spent 19 months in orbit and confirmed that much more hydrogen than originally thought was present in the shadowed lunar craters at the poles.

Scientists believe that the best explanation for so much hydrogen would be the presence of water ice. Some researchers suggested that comet fragments, which carry water ice, may have crashed into these areas in the past and the ice, hidden from the Sun's heat, remains frozen there.

When *Prospector's* mission was finished, engineers planned an impact with the Moon at the suspected site of some of this water ice. When the little satellite hit the surface, they hoped to see some sign of ice among the debris thrown up by the impact. The spacecraft was angled and aimed, and it seemed to crash as planned. However, no one spotted any evidence of an icy spray. So, unfortunately, the satellite's impact provided no further confirmation for this theory. Nevertheless, many scientists still think that water ice is probably the best explanation for the presence of so much hydrogen on the Moon.

Uncovering Venus

Venus, the "second rock from the Sun," is almost the same size as Earth. At one time, the two planets may have been very similar, but poisonous clouds of sulfuric acid now surround Venus. The planet's thick atmosphere hides its surface from viewers on Earth.

Several early orbiters launched by the Soviet Union and the United States explored the clouds and atmosphere of Venus, but none gave us a complete picture of what the surface was like. Then, in 1978, *Pioneer Venus* arrived at this nearby planet. For the next 14 years, the spacecraft orbited Venus and sent back photos and reams of data.

Radar equipment onboard *Pioneer Venus* provided scientists with a detailed overview of Venus's surface. The satellite sent out radar waves that zipped through the clouds to the surface and then bounced back to the spacecraft. By measuring the time it took for the waves to return, scientists determined the relative height of structures on the surface.

In 1989, astronauts onboard the Space Shuttle *Atlantis* launched another satellite to study Venus. Between 1990 and 1994, *Magellan* used extremely sophisticated radar equipment to map 98 percent of Venus's surface. It captured detail as small as a football field. For the first time, scientists saw volcanic lava flows, and quake faults, as well as a variety of unique features on this hot planet's surface.

An artist's conception of the *Magellan* spacecraft as it surveyed the planet Venus

An artist's conception of the *Mars Global Surveyor* as it orbits the Red Planet and maps its surface

Martian Chronicles

Mars has received many visits—and many more attempted visits—from spacecraft launched by the United States and the former Soviet Union. However, only two important satellite, or orbiter, missions have succeeded, the *Viking Orbiter 1* and *2* and *Mars Global Surveyor.*

When Mars enthusiasts think of the Viking mission, they usually think first of the two Viking landers that gave scientists their first ground-level view of Mars. However, high above the planet's surface the two *Viking Orbiter* spacecraft used color, stereo, and filtered images to help choose landing sites for the two landers. They also used their cameras to map the rest of the planet, dipping as close as 185 miles (298 km) to the surface to take a good look. The orbiters showed scientists that the north polar cap is composed almost entirely of water ice—a big surprise to Mars experts.

Twenty years later, headlines raved about the 1997 Mars Pathfinder mission and its robot rover *Sojourner*'s surface exploration on Mars. However, 2 years later, another important mission quietly

began its work overhead. *Mars Global Surveyor* was launched on November 6, 1996. The spacecraft arrived at Mars on September 11, 1997, and, after a time-out to adjust its orbit, began mapping the entire planet in 1999.

Mars Global Surveyor continues to provide valuable information about the Martian surface, atmosphere, and meteorology. In 1999 and

2000, scientists tried—without success—to use *Mars Global Surveyor* to find remnants of the *Mars Polar Lander,* a spacecraft lost just as it was landing on Mars in December 1999.

Mingling Among Jupiter's Moons

In the 1970s and early 1980s, four spacecraft—*Pioneer 11, Pioneer 12, Voyager 1,* and *Voyager 2*—flew by Jupiter and its moons. What scientists saw in these first close-up views was exciting. The spacecraft detected a faint ring around Jupiter that had not been seen from Earth, and they revealed some fascinating features on Jupiter's four big moons. Scientists decided to follow up these "fly-by" missions with an orbiting spacecraft, an artificial satellite called *Galileo.*

Galileo was launched from the Space Shuttle *Atlantis* in 1989 to take a closer look at all four of Jupiter's big moons. After a 6-year journey, the spacecraft arrived at Jupiter in 1995. There, it became a satellite as it entered orbit around the giant planet.

Io, the big moon closest to Jupiter, is a hotbed of volcanic activity. Scientists were able to adjust *Galileo*'s orbit around Jupiter to make several near passes and get close-up images of Io's volcanoes spewing molten material.

At the moon called Europa, *Galileo* discovered evidence of what may be a liquid ocean of water beneath a surface of thick, cracked water ice. This exciting possibility raised another big question: Could some form of life be hidden beneath Europa's ice?

On Ganymede, a moon larger than the planets Mercury and Pluto, *Galileo* found something very unusual—a magnetic field. No other moon in the solar system is known to have a magnetic field. Scientists were especially surprised by the find because Ganymede's magnetic field

An artist's conception of *Galileo* touring the large moons of Jupiter

exists within the strong magnetic field of Jupiter. "What we've found," said Galileo project scientist Torrance Johnson at the time, "is a magnetosphere within a magnetosphere."

However, the fourth moon, Callisto, held one of the biggest surprises. *Galileo* revealed that this heavily cratered moon may possess a salty liquid ocean far beneath its surface. As space physicist Margaret Kivelson remarked, "Until now, we thought Callisto was a dead and boring moon, just a hunk of rock and ice. . . . The new data certainly suggest that something is hidden below Callisto's surface, and that something may very well be a salty ocean." During its years orbiting among the moons of Jupiter, *Galileo* has provided scientists with a great deal to think about and enormous quantities of high-resolution images and data to explore.

Examining Saturn and Titan

The spacecraft *Cassini* left Earth for Saturn in 1997 and should arrive in 2004. There, it will orbit the ringed planet and pass by as many of Saturn's moons as it safely or reasonably can. (Some moons would be dangerous to visit because they orbit within the planet's rings. Others are much too far away to reach.)

As it flies for the first time past Titan, Saturn's biggest moon, *Cassini* will release a probe called *Huygens* that will parachute through

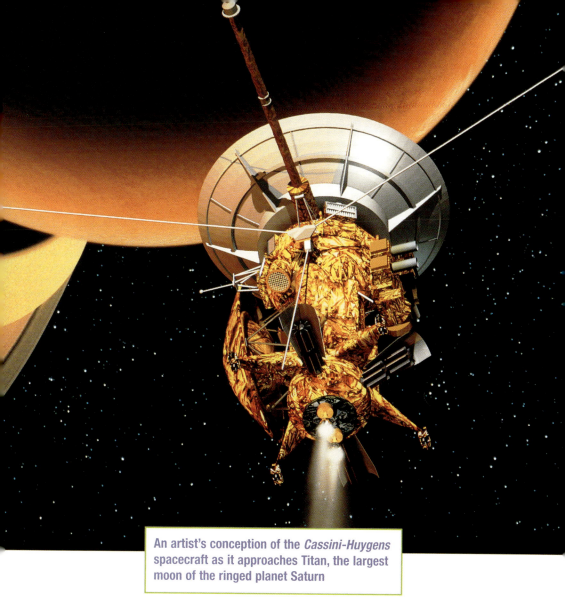

An artist's conception of the *Cassini-Huygens* spacecraft as it approaches Titan, the largest moon of the ringed planet Saturn

the atmosphere to the big moon's surface. The orbiting satellite will then keep in touch with *Huygens* and relay all the information the little probe collects back to Earth. Scientists expect this exciting mission to resolve countless mysteries about the rings of Saturn, many of its moons, and the planet itself.

Chapter 8

Satellite Dwellings

During the early years of the space race, a competition to put humans in space quickly became an important part of the contest. The Soviets were first to place a piloted spacecraft in orbit, when cosmonaut Yuri Gagarin became the first human in space in April 1961. John Glenn became the first American astronaut to orbit Earth in February 1962. These two men and all the others who orbited Earth after them aboard various spacecraft—including the early Soviet Vostok and Voskhod models and the U.S. Mercury and Gemini capsules—were actually traveling aboard satellites while they were in orbit.

Another kind of satellite can also carry people—space laboratories and space stations. The Space Shuttle, *Skylab*, the Soviet Salyut stations, *Mir,* and the *International Space Station* have all orbited, or currently orbit, Earth. They are all part of the past and present assortment of satellites in space.

Satellite Repair

The first official Space Shuttle flight took place in April 1981. The Space Shuttle fleet included several orbiters. The *Columbia* orbiter, piloted by astronauts John W. Young and Robert L. Crippen, made the first flight.

At the beginning of each flight, three external rocket boosters lift the big Space Shuttle into orbit and then fall away. Although launched by rocket, the shuttle is shaped like a giant airplane and lands on a runway. Not only is the Space Shuttle a satellite itself when it's in orbit, but it plays two important roles in the lives of other satellites that orbit our planet—satellite launching and satellite repair.

Many satellites are launched directly into orbit by rockets, much as *Sputnik* and *Explorer* were. However, more complex satellite launches are often shepherded into orbit by astronauts from the cargo bay of the Space Shuttle.

From the shuttle bay, astronauts have also floated out into space on intricate space walk missions to extend the lifetimes of some satellites with key repairs. Among the most spectacular of these missions have been the three that serviced and upgraded the *Hubble Space Telescope* (*HST*), launched in 1990.

The first *HST* repair mission took place in 1993, and as one *HST* mission scientist put it, "This is not a trip to Grandma's house to fix the faucet." The telescope's flawed primary mirror could be fixed, but

Astronauts onboard the Space Shuttle *Endeavour* made updates and repairs to the *Hubble Space Telescope*.

the job had to be done right or *HST* might never achieve its full potential. To do the job, the astronauts used the shuttle's remote manipulator system to position the 43-foot (13-m) telescope upright in the cargo bay. The entire repair mission, which involved installing a specially designed kit of corrective optics to compensate for the flawed mirror, took five *extravehicular activities* (*EVAs*) to complete. The astronauts also installed new gyroscopes, replaced the solar arrays (the wing-like structures that hold the solar cells that supply power to the satellite), replaced a scientific instrument and several electrical units, and performed other needed repairs. In 1997, another shuttle crew installed more new instruments and repaired the telescope's insulation.

Then, in November 1999, *HST* went into safe mode—it automatically turned off and covered its lens—when the third of its six gyroscopes shut down. The telescope needs at least three functioning gyroscopes to keep a steady focus on the objects it observes. If one more failed, *HST* would no longer be able to make observations.

So shuttle astronauts performed an update mission in December. They replaced all the gyroscopes, installed a faster main computer, and installed other new equipment to keep the satellite healthy. The job required three strenuous EVAs, each more than 8 hours long, but the mission was successful and took only 7 days. The *Hubble Space Telescope* was back in business, ready to continue its 20-year mission.

Living and Working in Orbit

Newspapers and television often play up the "big" jobs in space, such as building a space station, launching a satellite, or performing EVAs. However, payload and mission specialists aboard the shuttle

Wanted: Right the First Time

Before Catherine "Cady" Coleman became the lead mission specialist during the 1999 *Chandra X-ray Observatory* launch, she had already proved her ability to work well in space. She made her first shuttle trip in 1995 on the second U.S. Microgravity Laboratory (USML-2) mission.

At that time, Coleman was a captain in the Air Force and had a Ph.D. in polymer science and engineering. She has also set several NASA records for endurance and tolerance in EVA and microgravity training.

The Microgravity Laboratory mission was right up Coleman's alley. The astronauts would have to perform experiments in materials science, a field that Coleman already knew a lot about.

"The shuttle experiments are expensive, of course, and they can't easily be repeated," explains Tom McCarthy, who was Coleman's adviser in graduate school. "Cady has good hands in the lab, she does things right the first time."

Mission specialists Catherine "Cady" Coleman and Michel Tognini working together aboard the Space Shuttle *Columbia*

orbiters also run many other important experiments during their missions.

The shuttle bay is large enough to carry a full-sized scientific laboratory, and several missions have flown with such laboratories aboard. Many missions have also carried laser sensors, cameras, and other instruments for special Sun and Earth observations. Additionally, nearly all missions run some experiments in microgravity—testing the effects of weightlessness, or near-weightlessness, on various materials, on physical and biological processes, and on people.

Labs in the Sky

The unique spacecraft known as *Skylab* was the first U.S. space station—a small laboratory that was used for only 1 year. It was built from materials left over from NASA's Apollo Program, which sent a total of twelve astronauts to walk on the Moon. The main body was made from a converted *Saturn 4B* rocket, part of a spare *Saturn 5* booster designed to send the Apollo spacecraft on its lunar journey. Inside this empty cylinder, NASA built a cabin that had about 10,000 square feet (929 sq m) of living area.

Three separate crews lived and worked in *Skylab* as it orbited Earth in 1973. The astronauts performed life-science experiments, including a test to see how well a spider could spin a web in microgravity (just fine, after a few tries). They also took thousands of photographs of Earth and the Sun and performed extensive observations of the Sun. The *Skylab* missions represented the first U.S. experience with long-duration stays in space. The third crew set a record of 84 days that no one surpassed until 1978, when three Soviet cosmonauts onboard the *Salyut 6* space station outstayed them.

Between 1971 and 1982, the Soviet Union placed a series of Salyut space stations in orbit. Each one monitored the long-term physiological and psychological effects of living in space and housed many microgravity experiments. The last crew left *Salyut 7* in 1986, and the satellite plunged to Earth in 1991.

In 1986, the Soviet Union launched the space station *Mir*. This was by far the most ambitious of the Soviet space stations. Over its long life, engineers have added several modules for work and living. Astronauts from many nations visited *Mir* and worked in its laboratories. Between 1994 and 1999, after the Cold War ended, several U.S. astronauts joined Russian cosmonauts aboard *Mir*. Astronaut Shannon

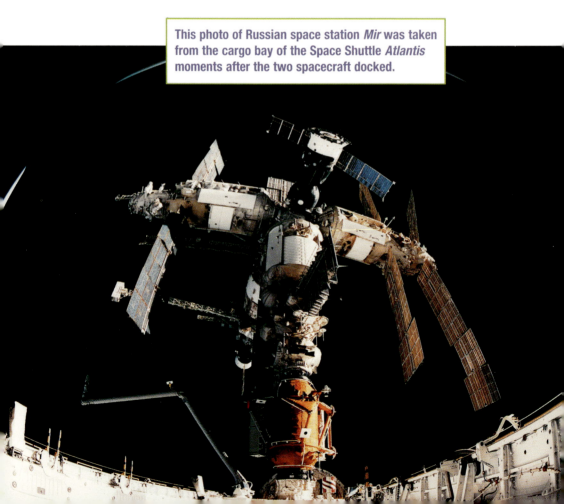

This photo of Russian space station *Mir* was taken from the cargo bay of the Space Shuttle *Atlantis* moments after the two spacecraft docked.

Lucid set an international endurance record for women during her stay of 188 days in space.

In the late 1990s, *Mir* suffered many mishaps. In 1997 especially, several crises occurred. First, a fire broke onboard the spacestation. Luckily, cosmonauts extinguished it quickly. Then an automated supply ferry, *Progress*, collided with the space station and punctured one of the science modules. A month later, a crew member accidentally moved a cable, causing the station to lose nearly all its power until the problem was repaired.

For all its difficulties, though, *Mir* has had a long, continuous presence in space—a tribute to human technological ability and perseverance.

A Permanent International Lab

Many people hope that the *International Space Station* (*ISS*) will succeed in picking up where *Mir* leaves off. The space station is the first orbiting microgravity laboratory built by a team of nations. High above Earth, it orbits at a dizzying 239 miles (384 km). After long planning and preparation, Space Shuttle astronauts put the first two modules in orbit in 1998 and joined them to form the first kernel of a new home in space. In July 2000, the Russians launched *Zveda*, a service module spacecraft that docked with ISS. The first crew arrived 3 months later.

The arrival came not a moment too soon. The orbit of *Mir* was beginning to deteriorate, and the big Russian space station was starting to show its age. The *International Space Station* could replace *Mir*, though, as a permanent habitat in space. It represents a new foothold for humans in space, a new island in orbit. It is also a new kind of

This artist's conception shows what the *International Space Station* will look like when it is complete. It will have a pressurized interior the size of two jumbo jets and will accommodate seven astronauts at a time.

workplace—one where scientific research and microgravity manufacturing can take place, conducted by international crews.

One day, the *International Space Station* may even become a stopover for crews on their way to more distant destinations, such as the Moon or Mars or the Martian moon Phobos.

Chapter 9

Higher than the Highest Mountain

nyone who has ever climbed a mountain knows that the higher you
go, the better the view, and the more you can see. Satellites have
given humanity a higher mountaintop to climb, to see farther and
more globally. The benefits are enormous.

Some critics warn that space junk is becoming a problem. Humans
have been lobbing pieces of metal and plastic into orbit for nearly 50
years, and many of the original satellites, although dead and useless,
continue to orbit Earth.

Luckily, a few relatively new ideas promise to help. We have
already begun to move failed or ailing satellites out of popular orbits
to make room for new ones. Shuttle crews have developed skills for

Landsat 4 is one of the many artificial satellites that have been launched into space.

repairing and retrieving satellites. In addition, engineers are designing a "savior satellite" that will be able to perform automated repairs on broken satellites.

In recent years, satellite data have become more available to everyone. Many of the images satellites have provided are now posted on the Internet. At one time, only experts who were trained in data analysis and had access to high-powered computers could use Landsat images. Today, though, new software makes these images available to people in a variety of professions.

New satellite image technology detects a large range of the light spectrum, and users can switch to the part of the spectrum that shows the details they are interested in. Newly designed software makes the images easy to use and understand, and it can be used on computers that people have in their offices and homes.

For example, engineers can examine local ground cover before designing a storm drainage system for a particular area. Military strategists can find out whether the terrain in a particular area will support heavy vehicles and tanks. Bankers who want to place a value on real estate property can see how the current owner's usage may affect its value. Schools and city planners can plot the best bus routes. Farmers can take a bird's-eye view of their fields and make sound decisions about fertilizer or crop rotation.

The satellite world is now more than ever part of everyday life and everyday business. New technologies constantly expand the sophistication and usefulness of satellites. Who can guess all the ways that they will be helping us and improving our lives 20 or 30 years from now?

Satellite Launches: A Timeline

1957	The Soviet Union puts the first artificial satellite, *Sputnik 1*, into Earth orbit.
	The Soviet Union launches *Sputnik 2* into Earth orbit.
1958	The United States successfully launches an artificial satellite, *Explorer 1*, into Earth orbit.
	NASA (National Aeronautics and Space Administration) begins operations.
1960	The United States launches *TIROS 1*, the first successful weather satellite.
	NASA launches *Echo 1*, first real communications satellite.
1962	*Telstar 1*, the first privately built satellite is launched.
	The Canadian satellite *Alouette 1* is launched.
1963	The final Mercury mission carries L. Gordon Cooper into space inside *Faith 7*.

1964	*Syncom 2*, the first geostationary telecommunications satellite is launched.
	Italy launches its first satellite, *San Marco 1*.
1965	France sends its first satellite, *Astérix*, into space.
1967	Australia launches its first satellite, *Wresat*.
1969	First astronauts land on the Moon.
	Germany sends its first satellite, *Azur*, into space.
1970	Japan and China each launch their first satellite into space.
1971	The United Kingdom launches its first satellite, *Prospero*.
1974	The first direct broadcasting satellite, *ATS 6*, is launched.
	The Netherlands and Sapin each launch their first satellite.
1975	India sends its first satellite, *Aryabhata*, into space.

1976	— Indonesia sends its first satellite, *Palapa A1*, into space.
1977	— The first Space Shuttle orbiter, *Enterprise*, is flown in tests atop a Boeing 747.
1978	— *Seasat A* begins global observations of the Earth's oceans.
	Czechoslovakia launches its first satellite, *Magion 1*.
1981	— First piloted flight of the Space Shuttle is made by *Columbia*.
	The first Bulgarian satellite, *Intercosmos 22*, is launched.
1983	— The European Space Agency (ESA) places two satellites in orbit with the first successful launch by an *Ariane 1* rocket.
1984	— The *Solar Maximum Mission* (*SMM*) becomes the first satellite repaired in orbit by shuttle astronauts.
	The first satellites are brought back from space aboard the Space Shuttle.

1985	— The first Brazilian satellite, *Brasilsat A1*, is launched.
	The first Mexican satellite, *Morelos 1*, is launched.
1986	— The Space Shuttle *Challenger* is destroyed, and its entire crew of seven is killed after an explosion 73 seconds into the flight. A long investigation and redesign process follows.
	The first Swedish satellite, *Viking*, is launched.
1988	— Israel launches its first satellite, *Offek 1*.
	The first satellite from Luxembourg, *Astra 1A*, is launched.
1990	— The first satellite from Argentina, *Lusat*, is launched.
	The *Hubble Space Telescope* is launched from the Space Shuttle.
	The first satellite from Pakistan, *Badr A*, is launched.
1992	— The first South Korean satellite, *Kitsat A*, is launched.

1993 — The first satellite from Portugal, *Posat*, is launched.

The first satellite from Thailand, *Thaicom 1*, is launched.

1994 — The first satellite from Turkey, *Turksat 1B*, is launched.

1995 — The first Ukrainian satellite, *Sich 1*, is launched. The first satellite from Chile, *Fasat Alfa*, is launched. *PanAmSat* provides first global satellite services from a civilian company.

1996 — The first Malaysian satellite, *Measat 1*, is launched.

1997 — The first satellite from the Philippines, *Mabuhay 1*, is launched.

1999 — *Chandra X-ray Observatory* is launched from the Space Shuttle.

Terra satellite is launched to monitor Earth's weather and climate.

Glossary

altimeter—an instrument that measures the height of points on land or sea compared to a base altitude, such as sea level

biosphere—the entire Earth, all the organisms that live here, and everything that makes life here possible

black hole—a theoretical invisible region of space that has such extreme gravity that nothing—including light—can escape from it

booster—an extra rocket (sometimes called a *booster rocket*) used to give an additional boost, or lift, to the main cargo and other rockets. As their fuel is used up, booster rockets are discarded and, depending on design, may either fall back to Earth or remain in orbit. Some empty booster rockets can be collected and reused.

chloroflurocarbon (CFC)—a synthetic chemical that blocks the formation of ozone in Earth's atmosphere

corona—the hot, thin outer atmosphere of the Sun

eccentric—describes the flatness of an ellipse

ecliptic plane—the plane in which all the planets orbit the Sun

electromagnetic spectrum—the full range of the waves and frequencies of electromagnetic radiation. Radio waves are the longest waves in the spectrum, then microwaves (including radar) and infrared rays. Visible light is about in the middle. On the short end of the spectrum are ultraviolet (UV) waves, X rays, and finally gamma rays.

El Niño (Spanish for "child")—a warm seasonal ocean current that runs southward along the coast of Peru. Every 4 to 5 years, this current extends farther south, raising water temperatures several degrees above normal.

extravehicular activity (EVA)—a space walk; activity outside a spacecraft

galaxy—an enormous grouping of stars, often disk-shaped

geostationary—relating to an artificial satellite that orbits above Earth's equator at the same speed as Earth, so that the satellite always remains above the same spot on Earth

geosynchronous—see geostationary

jettison—to cast off or discard

La Niña (*Spanish for "the girl child"*)—a seasonal ocean current that causes unusually cold temperatures in the region of the Pacific Ocean near the equator

microgravity—a condition in which the force of gravity is less than that on Earth's surface

momentum—a physical property of an object that determines how long it will continue to move when acted upon by a constant force

multistage rocket—a rocket system that uses one or more booster rockets to provide additional lift

nebula (*pl. nebulae*)—an immense body of gas or dust in space

orbit—the path an object follows as it revolves around another body in space

phytoplankton—one of a large group of microscopic plants that live in the ocean

pulsar—a relatively old star that give out pulses of radiation, mostly radio waves

reconnaissance satellite—a satellite that provides a detailed survey of a region, conducts surveillance, and gathers electronic information

satellite—an object that orbits another object. Natural satellites include planets, asteroids, or comets that orbit the Sun or a moon that orbits a planet or an asteroid. Many artificial satellites, such as the Sputnik satellite and Gemini spacecraft, have been launched into space by humans.

spectrometer—an instrument that separates different colors or waves from the energy (light) of a star or planet so that they can be studied apart from each other

supernova—a massive star that explodes suddenly at the end of its life, increasing its brightness by many billion times; the brightness gradually fades

transponder—a receiver that can also transmit on a programmed signal

To Find Out More

The news from space changes fast, so it's always a good idea to check the copyright date on books, CD-ROMs, and video tapes to make sure that you are getting up-to-date information. One good place to look for current information from NASA is U.S. government depository libraries. There are several in each state.

Books

Burrows, William. *This New Ocean: A History of the First Space Age.* New York: Random House, 1998.

Campbell, Ann Jeanette. *The New York Public Library Amazing Space: A Book of Answers for Kids.* New York: John Wiley & Sons, 1997.

Gavaghan, Helen. *Something New Under the Sun: Satellites and the Beginning of the Space Age.* New York: Springer-Verlag, 1998.

Schefter, James. *The Race: The Uncensored Story of How America Beat Russia to the Moon.* New York: Doubleday, 1999.

Spangenburg, Ray, and Diane Moser. *Exploring the Reaches of the Solar System.* New York: Facts On File, Inc., 1990.

Video Tape

History of Spaceflight: Reaching for the Stars. Finley-Holiday Film Corp., 1995.

Organizations and Online Sites

Many of the sites listed below are NASA sites, with links to many other interesting sources of information about artificial satellites. You can also sign up to receive NASA news on many subjects via e-mail.

Astronomical Society of the Pacific
http://www.aspsky.org
390 Ashton Avenue
San Francisco, CA 94112

The Astronomy Café
http://www2.ari.net/home/odenwald/cafe.html
NASA scientist Sten Odenwald answers questions and offers news and articles relating to astronomy and space.

Kennedy Space Center
http://www.ksc.nasa.gov/ksc.html
This site features an overview of shuttle flights as well as information about the Mercury, Gemini, and Apollo programs.

NASA Ask a Space Scientist
http://image.gsfc.nasa.gov/poetry/ask/askmag.html#list
NASA scientists answer your questions about astronomy, space, and space missions. The site also has archives and fact sheets.

NASA Human Spaceflight

http://spaceflight.nasa.gov/index-m.html

This is the Internet hub for exploring everything related to human spaceflight, including current stories and realtime data as they break. You can explore the *International Space Station*, track Space Shuttle flights, trace space history, and see many interesting images.

NASA Newsroom

http://www.nasa.gov/newsinfo/newsroom.html

This site has NASA's latest press releases, status reports, and fact sheets. It includes a NASA News Archive for past reports and a search button for the NASA Web. You can even sign up for e-mail versions of all NASA press releases.

NASDA (National Space Center of Japan)
Cosmic Information Center

http://spaceboy.nasda.go.jp/index_e.html

Select "Space Notes" at the Cosmic Information Center home page and then select "Artificial Satellites" to open up a wealth of information about satellites and how they work.

National Space Society

http://www.nss.org
600 Pennsylvania Avenue, S.E., Suite 201
Washington, DC 20003

The Planetary Society
http://www.planetary.org/
65 North Catalina Avenue
Pasadena, CA 91106-2301

The Tech Museum Satellite Site
http://www.thetech.org/hyper/satellite/
The online site of the Tech Museum in San Jose, California, is sponsored by Lockheed Martin, a major satellite designer and manufacturer. Click on "What is a satellite, anyway?", "What do satellites do?", "Satellite Anatomy," or "Satellite Orbits." You'll also find instructions for building models of three kinds of satellites and news about satellites under the topic "Satellite of the Month."

Places to Visit

Check the Internet (*www.skypub.com* is a good place to start), your local visitors' center, or phone directory for planetariums and science museums near you. Here are a few suggestions:

Exploratorium
3601 Lyon Street
San Francisco, CA 94123
http://www.exploratorium.edu/
Internationally acclaimed interactive science exhibits, including astronomy subjects.

Space Center Houston

Space Center Houston Information
1601 NASA Road 1
Houston, TX 77058
http://www.spacecenter.org/
Offers a tour and exhibits related to humans in space, including the Apollo missions to the Moon.

Jet Propulsion Laboratory (JPL)

4800 Oak Grove Drive
Pasadena, CA 91109
http://www.jpl.nasa.govk/faq/#tour
Tours available once or twice a week by arrangement; see web site for instructions, or call or write to the JPL visitor contact. JPL is the primary mission center for all NASA planetary missions.

NASA Goddard Space Flight Center

Code 130, Public Affairs Office
Greenbelt, MD 20771
http://www.pao.gsfc.nasa.gov/vc/info/info.htm
Visitors can see a Moon Rock, brought back to Earth by Apollo astronauts, as well as other related exhibits.

The Tech Museum of Innovation
201 South Market Street
San Jose, CA 95113-2008
http://www.thetech.org/
Offers more than 240 interactive exhibits featuring high-tech technology. Permanent exhibits include "Communications: Global Communications," "Exploration: New Frontiers," "Innovation: Silicon Valley and Beyond," "Life Tech: The Human Machine," and "The Spirit of American Innovation," honoring recipients of the National Medal of Technology.

Index

Bold numbers indicate illustrations.

About the Authors

Ray Spangenburg and **Kit Moser** are a husband-and-wife writing team specializing in science and technology. They have written 38 books and more than 100 articles, including a five-book series on the history of science and a four-book series on the history of space exploration. As journalists, they covered NASA and related science activities for many years. They have flown on NASA's Kuiper Airborne Observatory, covered stories at the Deep Space Network in the Mojave Desert, and experienced zero-gravity on experimental NASA flights out of NASA Ames Research Center. They live in Carmichael, California, with their two dogs, Mencken (a Sharpei mix) and F. Scott Fitz (a Boston Terrier).